RESPONSES TO THE WHITE PAPER

RESPONSES TO THE WHITE PAPER

Edited by Wilf Stevenson and Nick Smedley

BFI Publishing

First published in 1989 by the
British Film Institute
21 Stephen Street
London W1P 1PL

Copyright © British Film Institute 1989

British Library Cataloguing in Publication Data
Responses to the White Paper. – (The broadcasting
    debate).
    1. Great Britain. Broadcasting services
    I. Stevenson, Wilfrid   II. Smedley, Nick
    III. British Film Institute   IV. Series
    384.54'0941

ISBN 0–85170–253–8

Cover design: Julia King

Typeset in 10 on 11½pt Sabon by
Fakenham Photosetting Limited, Fakenham, Norfolk
Printed by
St Edmundsbury Press, Bury St Edmunds, Suffolk

Contents

Introduction

This booklet aims to present a broad overview of some of the main submissions sent to the Government in response to its White Paper, 'Broadcasting in the '90s: Competition, Choice and Quality'. The booklet does not claim to be a comprehensive précis of the 3,000 or so submissions received by the Home Office. It attempts to capture the mood of a significant slice of those submissions, reflecting a cross-section of the major interested parties – broadcasting bodies, television and radio companies, producers, consumer groups, trade unions, advertisers and so on. We have not sought to balance every expression of view with an opposite point of view but instead have attempted to present the main trends in the evidence and the majority response; where, however, significant players have expressed directly countervailing views to the majority opinion, we have attempted to reflect that too.

The method we have chosen is to summarise briefly at the start of each chapter first the Government's proposals, and then the prevailing trends of the evidence we reviewed. After this, we have chosen to let the submissions speak for themselves, using pertinent quotations from the evidence, linked by very brief passages of our own. Inevitably, the use of quotations to illustrate a mass of often quite detailed evidence is a highly selective process; unless clearly stated otherwise, any quote or group of quotes has been chosen not only for its succinctness but also for its representativeness.

Finally, it will be apparent that much of what follows is critical of the Government's proposals. This is not a result of our adopting a partisan approach to those proposals. The BFI has no significant self-interest in the debate and has not sought to promote any specific response to the Government's plans. Rather, the tone of the document which follows is a genuine reflection of the strength of critical opposition to the White Paper to be found in the evidence we reviewed. It is perhaps inevitable, in any event, that responses to a White Paper are going to expend more time and energy on those aspects with which they profoundly disagree and where they thus seek to change the Government's mind, than on those parts where they and others are in accord with what is proposed.

1
The Political Background

The White Paper 'Broadcasting in the '90s: Competition, Choice and Quality' has had a long genesis. The Peacock Report, published in July 1986, was perhaps the immediate starting point. Although it was not entirely accepted by the Government, many observers felt that legislation would rapidly follow. In the event, the White Paper did not appear until November 1988, with legislation scheduled for the 1989–90 Parliamentary Session.

The Peacock Committee had been set up in March 1985 to review the financing of the BBC. Its terms of reference required it to consider only the consequences of introducing advertising or sponsorship into the BBC, following a sustained campaign from advertisers and free-market pressure groups (e.g. the Adam Smith Institute). In the event, however, the Committee made recommendations covering the future structure of broadcasting more generally, on the grounds that it would make no sense to consider the BBC in isolation from the rest of the broadcasting market.

The Committee's key recommendations were as follows:

- There should be no advertising on the BBC while the present structure of broadcasting remained;
- the licence fee should be indexed to the RPI;
- the BBC should collect the fee;
- a split recommendation about the extent to which Radios 1 and 2 should be privatised;
- 40 per cent of programmes on both the BBC and ITV should be commissioned from independent producers within 10 years;
- the night hours should be sold off (this included both the BBC and ITV);

3

- a split recommendation (4 to 3) on selling franchises to the highest bidder, with those in favour still accepting that the option *not* to sell to the highest bidder must remain, but that reasons must be stated; the dissenters argued that such a system was unacceptable;
- Channel 4 to have the option of selling its own advertising;
- the obscenity laws to be extended to broadcasting once regulation is phased out.

The Committee went on to propose a long-term evolution towards subscription, with a Public Service Broadcasting Council to maintain standards. It also suggested a single transmission authority should be set up in the long term. Its overall aim was stated to be to secure direct consumer choice on the BBC rather than the universal licence fee. The Report was an attempt to bridge the gap between realisation of that aim and the existing arrangements.

The Government took no action following the Report's publication. With the benefit of hindsight, this delay may have helped rather than hindered the drafters of the White Paper, for in the interim the market for satellite channels emerged, and studies on various technological developments, such as MVDS and the spectrum problems affecting Channel 5, were completed. The Government's announcement in November 1987 of its intention to introduce broadcasting legislation prompted the Home Affairs Committee to conduct its own enquiries, resulting in the publication of a far-reaching and influential document, 'The Future of Broadcasting' (H.A.C., 3rd Report, session 1987–88) in June 1988.

This review was widely applauded on its appearance for, while it did not duck all the challenges of the changing broadcasting environment, it offered a robust defence of the present system of public service broadcasting. Key points included:

para 18: 'From our international discussions we have come to appreciate that, whatever criticisms are made legitimately at home, abroad British television is seen to be amongst the best, if not the best, in the world. British broadcasters have set standards across the whole range of television programmes that we would wish to see maintained.'

para 23: 'To discard the very factors which have contributed to the universal esteem in which British broadcasting has been held would clearly be unwise and arguably unnecessary.'

para 24: '... the principles of public service broadcasting should be an integral part of the new broadcasting environment.'

para 34: 'We will look to the established channels to continue to expand their output to meet the needs of minority communities.'

paras 42–3: The Committee argued that safeguards against concentration of ownership are needed.

para 51: 'All possible developments to expand consumer choice should be investigated while ensuring that future developments are not permitted at the expense of services currently received free of charge (sic).'

para 91: The Committee said that regulation will not be made redundant by multiple channels because 1) for most people things will not change yet; 2) market-led programming will not maintain diversity, information and education.

paras 115, 117: The Broadcasting Standards Council must '... base its role in a changing broadcasting environment on properly researched findings.'

para 128: '... in the medium term at least, the BBC should continue to be financed by means of the licence fee indexed to the retail price index.'

para 134: The Committee were in favour of abolishing the ITV levy, arguing that it should be replaced by a 'suitably regulated tendering process' aimed at securing high standards.

para 139: 'Channel 4 should remain substantially as it is at present. For the time being the current system of financing would seem to be the best method of achieving this end.'

para 171: The Committee stressed the importance of maintaining the regional nature of franchises after 1993.

para 173: The Committee favoured letting the ITV night hours as one, national separate franchise.

para 192: '... television can all too easily become dominated by the need to deliver audiences to advertisers rather than offering programmes to viewers. It is important to retain, in parts at least of the television system, the ethos of high quality television that has been the hall mark of BBC and Independent Television.'

When the Government published its White Paper in November

1988, it became clear that it had rejected a number of essential recommendations made by Peacock and by the Home Affairs Committee. Broadly speaking, the White Paper ignored Peacock's recommendation for the criteria determining the franchise auctions, while it departed from the Home Affairs Committee on a number of issues, including free, universal access to public service television; on the need for a stringent regulatory framework; on the need to protect the BBC's finances; on tendering for Channel 3 franchises; on the abolition of the levy; and on the future ownership of Channel 4.

Given the fact that the White Paper had gone against both these reports in key areas, it was perhaps not surprising that the subsequent Parliamentary debates – in both Houses – contained critical comments. What was surprising perhaps was the virtually unanimous opposition to the Government's proposals from all sides of the House and in both Chambers.

The House of Lords debate took place on 13 December 1988. The key points were:

The Minister of State, Home Office (Earl Ferrers): col 838 – 'The philosophy which has lain behind all the Government's considerations of what is a very wide and high technical subject is that the viewer and the listener are the ones who matter. In short, it is that people should have a wider choice and a greater say over what they watch and what they listen to. There are other matters of great importance, but they are secondary to that overriding philosophy.

What the Government is seeking to do is to acknowledge that conditions have changed; that new technologies are here and, as a result, that new possibilities have come about; and then to say, "Let us now create a framework in which radio and television can operate to the best of their abilities, and for the benefit of the public, with the facilities which are at their disposal."

The Government's duty, as we see it, is to create the framework within which enterprise, opportunity and consumer demand will determine what is available.'

Baroness Birk: col 844 – 'Yes, we shall have more competition. But there is a risk that it will be competition for mass audiences to please advertisers. Experience abroad shows that such competition inevitably leads to a flight down-market. Yes, we shall have more choice. But it will be a choice of many channels rather than a choice of different kinds of programming.

First, the Government propose that the award of franchises in

6

the ITV regions, which will be Channel 3, will be decided by auction, with the licences awarded to the highest bidders. This system will remove the incentive for ITV to maintain high standards, since all a successful bidder will need – in spite of what the Minister said so engagingly – is some pretty slender promises about quality and a very large capital outlay. How can a system like this possibly encourage choice and quality?

I fear that this Government is using technology as a means of imposing their ideology on broadcasting. But no technological revolution justifies uprooting so wantonly the product of gradual, thoughtful and extremely successful evolution.'

Lord Bonham-Carter: cols 848–9 – 'In my view, the White Paper is largely window-dressing. It is a display made in such a way as to give a falsely favourable impression of the facts. Behind the window-dressing the intention seems to me to be transparently obvious. It is ideological and political. The ideology is yet another obeisance to the market place. The political element is to gerry-mander the control and the ownership of television in this country. The purpose is to produce an ownership of television much like the ownership of the press; that is, overwhelmingly controlled by the supporters of the present Government.'

Bishop of St. Albans: col 853 – 'It simply will not do to leave quality broadcasting to good intention, to a free-for-all in the market place or to retrospective finger-wagging with a combi-nation of yellow and red cards. That has not done a noticeable amount of good for association football.'

Lord Barnett: cols 863–4 – 'Only two subscription services in the world make real money – Home Box Office in America, which provides a service of feature films uninterrupted by advertising, which in America is not available on other channels, and Canal Plus, in France, which provides mainly feature films, some of them peculiarly French. However, both BSB and Rupert Murdoch have already announced that they will each offer a premium film service on subscription in this country. I wish them well. But how will subscription develop for satellite, for parts of ITV, for Channel 5 or for the BBC? Only time will tell. However, of one thing I am sure – the funding system that succeeds will be the one that is most convenient and cost effective for the national audience.

We should nevertheless acknowledge the benefits of the licence fee. Because it is collected from the national audience the cost to individual households is low; namely, £1.20 a week. It enables the BBC to produce high-quality programming for all, regardless of wealth, wherever you live, right across the nation.'

Lord Annan: col 886 – 'As I read the Paper an image began to stain my imagination. I saw the Secretary of State for Home Affairs saying to TV Britannia: "Never fear, my dear, I will not let that gang of tycoons running satellite and other TV controls hurt you. Look at the safeguards I have provided; look at Lord Rees-Mogg who is there to preserve you from sexual assault and from violence. Look at the quality tests. What is more, I have kept their hands off the BBC, which will continue to be the flagship of public service broadcasting."

Then I heard from the screen the voice-over of the Secretary of State for Trade and Industry which we know so well in this house. It is so beguiling, so full of charm, so insistent that competition is always sound common sense. I heard him saying to TV Britannia: "You are going to be raped anyway, so why not lie back and enjoy it. You will have a wonderful choice of lovers."

Two ideas dominate the Department of Trade and Industry, and two ideas only. The first is how to get the maximum revenue out of television for the Exchequer, mainly of course by auctioning franchises, and by a levy based on income. The second is how to reduce the cost to advertisers and hence to business and industry, mainly by competition.

But if one sets up a body, the ITC, to regulate domestic commercial television, why not trust it? Why forbid it expressly, which Peacock did not, to judge between rival bids? Why compel the ITC to accept the highest bid even if it knows, and the informed public also knows, that the highest bidder is either a crook or a shark who will do his best to evade every control and peddle trash?'

Lord Willis: col 872 – 'A look at the future of broadcasting it may be; a blueprint for the future it most certainly ain't.

We have built a television system that is a model for the world. How can we prevent that system sinking under the weight of competition from these new aerial invaders? Instead of taking the sensible and ultimately commercial approach, the White Paper proposes, in effect, that we should take the opportunity to dig up the entire garden, roses and all, sack the gardeners and then wait to see what comes up.'

8

Lord Swann: col 878 – 'I rather suspect that we shall see the early demise of Channel Four as we know it. What about the BBC? Will we see a rerun of what happened in the 1950s, with political clamour for an end to the licence fee and hence an end to the BBC? For let there be no misunderstanding. The Peacock Committee was quite clear, following investigations by commercial and academic consultants, that advertising could not support both independent television, as it then stood, and the BBC, except conceivably if proposals were introduced very slowly and over a long period of time.'

Lord Orr-Ewing: cols 885–6 – 'I do not think it is right to say that "more" automatically means "worse". We had all these arguments when I first came into this Chamber in 1950 and noble Lords were having a debate. Lord Reith and all his chaps were present. It was going to be Gresham's law which would drive out everything and we should all be down in the gutter of the lowest common denominator of entertainment. It has not happened – we found the right formula – and it will not happen. I do not think that "more" means "worse"; it means "different". I hope that it means more choice.

The House will remember that we have four-year elections: 1995 will be the last year of whatever government is in power, so I do not think that they will start re-hashing the whole game again. If this were sacrosanct it may be difficult to change. I do not believe that it is beyond the wit of human beings or the will of the Government to adjust the licence and the charter to make sure that in future the BBC is no longer the judge, the jury and sometimes the gaoler in its own cause. It would stand in even greater reputation if it had an independent authority above it.

It is the person who can tell the tallest story and who has the longest purse who will win a franchise. That will not produce the balance of programmes we need. I know that it is tempting to say that this is a market economy. It is not. In the case of these programmes going into millions of homes we want to see high standards. I do not believe that we shall do any good by tearing up this mature plant, sacking the people, changing the whole thing and handing it over.'

Lord Blease: cols 890–2 – 'If profit is to be the primary motive, as it must be, for companies which have invested heavily in order to obtain franchises, the public service element of broadcasting must

9

find it difficult to survive. Quality programmes, whether drama or documentary, cost big money, while game shows and similar productions are much cheaper. Therefore it is inevitable that standards will decline. It is difficult to see how under such circumstances the proposed regulatory body with a light touch can effectively stand up to the pressures to lower standards in order to preserve the financial interests of the market.'

Lord Bishop of Winchester: col 892 – 'To my mind the thrust of the new proposals goes all out to maximise audiences – audiences with money to spend to satisfy the advertisers. The ITC will have no responsibility for scheduling as does the IBA at present. We have already been warned by the programme controllers at Thames Television and London Weekend that increased competition means the likely demise of children's programmes, arts programmes and religious programmes as well as current affairs. Therefore, I do not believe that it is sufficient for the White Paper to say that quality programmes will be available, although at a cost, for the specially targeted audience. Public service broadcasting has provided quality programmes to a wide audience as a right – not by imposing charges for their quality and not by demanding that viewers should subscribe.'

Viscount Ridley: cols 894–6 – 'I come from the North-East. Our staple diet of brown ale has been, or is likely to be, taken over by the Australians. Our last shipyard closed this week and there is a threat over the armaments industry at Vickers. Therefore, I hope that we will fight to retain our regional TV if that is all that is left. There must be built-in safeguards to that effect.

I know that in paragraph 6.11 there is a regional commitment, but it refers only to regional programmes. So far as that goes, it is good enough; but in my view it is equally, or even more important that ownership of the TV stations remains in regional hands which will represent a total commitment to the regions and all that goes with it. If the philosophy – which it is – of this Government is to make the regions more responsible and self-reliant, then the threat of losing regional TV seems to be undermining that policy already.

If auctioning franchises is to be adopted, why is it necessary to totally ignore the Peacock recommendation and say that the highest bid must be accepted? Taking the highest bid, whatever it may be, will be the greatest threat to the survival of the regional and smaller TV stations. The ability to accept a lower bid, as recommended by Peacock, is absolutely vital to the powers of the new ITC. Without it, and with the absence of any power to prevent takeovers, will the ITC have any power in practice? I wonder.'

Lord Taylor of Gryfe: col 897 – 'It is proposed that the transmission system be clarified and that there should be no cross-subsidisation such as enables independent television to reach the remotest corners of the country. Paradoxically, the largest and richest area (namely, London) requires the smallest number of transmitters. The distant parts of the country need several times that number in order to carry their broadcasts. Nothing in the White Paper indicates that arrangements will be made for this kind of cross-subsidisation which permits the regional companies to undertake these obligations in the future.'

Lord Harmar-Nichols: col 903 – 'When we talk about British television being the best in the world – indeed, in no other country have I been as impressed as I am with the quality and general scope of British TV – we ought to remember that the ITV companies have contributed to that great reputation. It is not only the BBC that has made the world think that we are reasonably good at this; it is also the result of the contribution made as much by the ITV companies, and in many ways more so.'

Lord Graham of Edmonton: cols 905–6 – 'The strategy has clearly been formulated with the interests of broadcasting consumers in mind. Unfortunately, those consumers are the advertising industry; in no sense whatsoever did the White Paper seriously reflect or advance viewers' interests.

Given the potential impact of the White Paper's proposals, it is remarkably lacking in serious economic analysis. It fails completely to address the issue of whether sufficient resources, especially advertising revenue, will be available to support the new free market in broadcasting.'

Lord Colwyn: col 909 – 'With a few reservations, I welcome this White Paper. I am sure that its basic principle is correct, that consumers should be able to choose which television service they wish to enjoy, and that, as far as possible, the provision of those services should be determined by normal market forces.

However, I also believe that certain key proposals will seriously endanger the prospect of achieving the Government's basic objectives. The combination of putting the Channel 3 licences out to tender, the proposed progressive levy, and the separation of Channel 4 from Channel 3 will so damage the economic base of Channel 3 that the service it is able to provide will be fundamentally changed. The most likely result will be the effective restoration of the BBC monopoly, and the loss both of any serious alternative news service and of a meaningful regional programme service.'

Lord Ardwick: cols 917–8 – 'Like everybody who has spoken today – everybody – I am appalled by the prospect of an auction for the franchises. It is true that the aspirants will have to show that they have the best of intentions about their programmes and only when they have passed the test will the bidding begin. It has been compared mockingly with a beauty contest after which the successful contestants will have to enter a second round in which they will be judged by the size of their dowries.

Let the Government stop pretending that the interests of commercial television companies and advertising agents are always the same as the interests of the people. They are not. Let them consider their timing. Could they not defer legislation until the four channels have learned to compete with the satellite operators?

The Conservatives at present stand in danger of going down in history as the government who created and inherited a system of British broadcasting which was the envy of the world and yet allowed it to be wrecked.'

Despite several requests to debate the White Paper shortly after its appearance, the House of Commons debate did not take place until 8 February 1989. The key points were:

Douglas Hurd: cols 1011–2 – 'Competitive tender, as the Peacock Committee said, is an inherently fairer and more objective procedure, which would also secure a proper return for the taxpayer in the use of a scarce resource. It is wrong to describe it simply as an auctioning of licences because that ignores the quality hurdle, which I have described. I know that the new chairman of the IBA, Mr George Russell, is looking carefully at the interaction of the two concepts of the quality hurdle and the competitive tender. We believe that both are essential – this is an important point – but the exact way in which we ask the ITC to operate them is a matter on which we shall listen carefully to the advice that he and many others may give.'

Roy Hattersley: cols 1091, 1022–4 – 'The White Paper gives absolutely no assurance that real choice – a choice between genuinely different types of programme – will be more available under the new scheme than at present. Standards fall without choice, in any real sense, being increased.

By forcing Channel 4 into direct competition for advertising with Channel 3, the Government will reduce the prospect of preserving Channel 4's distinctive character. When television is directly financed by advertising, its programmes and programme schedules, inevitably, are in part advertising-led. At present, because Channel 4 obtains its revenue from other independent companies, it does not need to concern itself with the type of programmes particularly favoured by dog food manufacturers and by junk food producers, but once Channel 4 is out on its own in the advertising market it will be forced to listen to their views – as Channel 3 openly admits that it is forced to do now. The result will be a Channel 4 which is more like Channel 3. Once again, there will be less choice, not more.

The Home Secretary is in part responsible for the confusion over the licence fee and its proper role in financing broadcasting. There was a great deal of speculation about its future before the White Paper was published, and the Home Secretary encouraged the nation with the delphic, indeed mystical, comment that the licence fee was "not immortal". As things now stand, the fee is not to have its throat cut suddenly but is to be slowly strangled. We have no doubt that the end of the fee would mark the end of public broadcasting.'

John Wheeler: cols 1027–9 – 'Our major report was published some four months before the White Paper, and the Committee must be gratified at the extent to which so many of its recommendations and conclusions have been adopted by the Government, even if the emphasis of the White Paper is not always the same as our own.

A particular matter in the White Paper which the Committee did not envisage was the proposed allocation to a commercial contractor of night-time hours on one of the BBC channels. In our report we went as far as to say that this was "totally unrealistic". When we took concluding evidence in May from the Minister of State, no hint of this possibility was given to us. I am afraid that in this proposal, the White Paper faces both ways at once. It exhorts the

BBC to raise money through subscription and then proposes that one possible outlet for such services – the night hours on one channel – is to be removed. If we are serious about wishing the BBC to use subscription finance in support of its income and to become financially more efficient, we should allow the BBC to retain its night hours to develop subscription services such as British medical television and a "BBC Nature Club". Three other terrestrial and countless satellite channels will be available to advertisers.'

Alick Buchanan-Smith: cols 1033–5 – 'If we are to have regional Channel 3 companies, and particularly if we are to maintain, as I believe we should, the small companies in the big geographic areas, transmission costs will be critical if they are to survive. One transmitter at Crystal Palace serves many millions of people in London. The Grampian area in the north of Scotland has 1.13 million inhabitants and is as large as Switzerland. Eight main transmitters and 68 relay transmitters are required to reach the population.

I remind my right hon. and hon. Friends that we have to watch the danger of putting profit before quality, particularly in regard to some of the smaller franchises.

I believe that there are also broader issues. Channels 3 and 4 being linked and working together provide a balance, because of a similar link between Channels 1 and 2 of the BBC. I believe that to have Channels 3 and 4 in the commercial sector and Channels 1 and 2 of the BBC linked not only provides a better balance but, if they are not linked, we shall lose the advantages of the complementary programming in the commercial sector which I believe helps viewers' choice.

Secondly, I should like to pay tribute to the success of S4C in Wales in relation to the Welsh language. I do not want to belittle what has been done elsewhere, but a company such as Grampian must provide Gaelic programmes and also contribute financially and directly to S4C in Wales. Why can we not have the same funding for Gaelic programmes as does S4C, which the White Paper has acknowledged has been a proven success?'

Robert Maclennan: cols 1036–8 – 'The White Paper rarely refers to the viewer and appears transfixed by two financial objectives of marginal benefit to the viewer. The first is to raise the maximum revenue for the Treasury by the sale of franchises and a levy based on income. The second is how to reduce costs to advertisers

14

through extended competition.

On competition, too, the White Paper is gravely defective. The Government appear to be bull-headed in their determination to stick to a tendering system of franchise allocation. I think that at best that is daft and at worst it is sinister. The Government has allowed a dangerous concentration of newspaper ownership in this country, but at least in that case there is always some possibility of a new entrant spotting a new market. As television franchises will be granted for many years the dangers of cross-ownership are far more serious. Television is also a much more pervasive medium than newspapers.

The White Paper that the Government ask us to endorse contains no adequate safeguards to prevent the domination of the networks by those with deep pockets and shallow concerns for freedom of expression and the virtues of diversity. The prospect that those who pay the piper in the press will also pay the piper across the airwaves induces revulsion and fear. The impact of the tendering arrangements and the role of the proposed licensing authority on the quality of programming will not be benign, even if the Home Secretary prevents the ownership of television channels by the press moguls. I believe that such ownership should be prevented.'

Jack Ashley: col 1042 – 'All the fine words in the White Paper about the BBC's special role and its high quality programmes cannot disguise the harsh fact that the BBC will be deprived of the cash that it needs to continue. The licence fee will be squeezed until 1991, and after that the Government clearly want to replace it with subscription television. That is like trying to run a Chieftain tank on lighter fuel – it simply will not work.'

Sir Geoffrey Pattie: cols 1044–5 – 'There is a danger that in the desire for choice, the Government is confusing qualitative choice with a mere proliferation in the number of channels. A large number of channels putting out American and Australian chat shows, which are largely indistinguishable from each other, do not meet my criteria for genuine choice. The provision – or at least the possibility of provision – of quality on our televisions is essential and that is much more likely to come from the selection of franchisees who meet the criteria and put in a good bid, but not necessarily the highest bid. We must remind ourselves that we and the Government act as trustees as much of our culture as of our

15

physical environment.

The one major omission of the White Paper concerns training. It is one of the critically important subjects about which one does not need to say a great deal because all hon. Members apparently recognise it when we see it. As my right hon. Friend the Prime Minister said in November 1988: It is impossible to overemphasise the importance of training. Training must be provided by the employers, but to be absolutely blunt about it, it will be provided only if the employers are required to provide it. Such a requirement should be inserted in the process at the quality threshold stage when would-be franchisees are running about making all the appropriate noises.'

Bruce Grocott: col 1051 – 'An extremely important factor about our television system is its universality. At a very simple level for people who, like me, are interested in sport, the great national sporting events such as test matches, cup finals, snooker finals and the Grand National are available to all nationwide. They are not on subscription or available only to the few. We should be taking a terrible step in the wrong direction if we made those sporting events available only on subscription channels so that they were not available universally.

The Home Secretary believes that the new system will be like browsing through a good bookshop. We shall refer to that phrase again and again as the new system evolves, but I fear that it will be far less like browsing through a good bookshop and more like browsing through a tatty newsagents.'

Roger Gale: cols 1056, 1058 – 'It saddens me that so many see those new circumstances as a threat. I see them as a tremendous opportunity for programme makers – as a programme maker myself – and for specialist channels showing education, religion, children's programmes, sport and films. The faint-hearted say that there is not the revenue to support all that – that we have an audience of only 50 million people – but we are looking at a potential audience for tomorrow's television companies of more than 500 million people throughout Europe. That is the audience that we should pitch at.

I welcome the White Paper as a formidable piece of work. I believe, and am delighted, that it reflects much of the unanimous report of the Select Committee on Home Affairs, and much of the sterling work done by Professor Sir Alan Peacock. I particularly

16

welcome the commitment to public service broadcasting which I believe the White Paper contains.

The White Paper has created a framework that is all right for terrestrial broadcasting. It meets some of the needs for transfrontier satellite entertainment and news. However, the White Paper falls short of creating a framework for total communications systems in the 21st century. I urge the Government to reconsider their decision to introduce a television authority and instead to introduce a total telecommunications authority that would embrace every sector. If we had that, I believe that we could beat the world.'

Margaret Ewing: col 1059 – 'There are many television production jobs in Scotland, but they are under threat. That applies, too, to production centres in Birmingham, Norwich, Manchester and elsewhere. If production centres are abolished, job opportunities will be lost. The talented men and women who work in production may find other opportunities in London or elsewhere. However, many of the people who are involved in network production at regional centres are committed to living and working there. They wish to stay in the regions. We do not want local skills to be lost. The ability to produce programmes locally means that Scottish actors are employed. That is important for repertory theatres. Local productions also employ musicians, which is important. It would be very sad if, at best, Scotland retained only one independent company and if, at worst, all control were to be removed from Scotland. I hope that the Home Office will respond positively to what I have said.'

George Walden: cols 1061–2 – 'The White Paper shows a total lack of social imagination, of what it means to be faced in one of our inner cities with a combination of low education provision and expectations and bad to mediocre teachers. On top of that, we propose to give people low expectations from teachers who will go home to another five hours of low expectations from television. I hope that those expectations will not be lowered, but evidence from the Government suggests otherwise.

There is a great danger in this country that when we get an idea we go on and on with it. We did that with egalitarianism and caused the damage that we now all know about. Now we have a new idea called market forces, and like children with a pot of paint we daub it all over the damned place. If we do that in broadcasting

17

or in education, we shall cause infinite damage to the people least well placed to support it.

It would be a dismal comment on a liberal Home Secretary to be seen in ten years' time as the man who introduced this tawdry debasement of our broadcasting system, with all the impact that it may have on social values of every kind.'

Robin Corbett: col 1069–72 – 'In the White Paper, any specific obligation of public service goes out of the window. That is because the Government simply want to hand over ITV to the men with the deepest pockets who will meet a so-called quality threshold no higher than a pile of £50 notes. Why do the Government not learn? Do they not remember that a previous Conservative Home Secretary, Lord Whitelaw, recognised when Channel 4 began that while financial resources without talent cannot provide quality television, neither can talent without financial resources? Lord Whitelaw built upon what was already in place. The present Home Secretary wants to do a demolition job.

The Government's approach throughout the White Paper is careless. Not for them any attempt to build on the basis of success, as would have been sensible for terrestrial broadcasting faced with massive competition from satellites. Not for them a planned advance adding to our present mix. No – they prefer the bulldozer to the bricklayer. What they plan will turn broadcasting inside out for no better reason than that it is a way to make a few quid for the Treasury.

It is not the so-called market value of a franchise which should guide the Government if they have the genuine interests of viewers and listeners at heart. It should be the quality and diversity of the content, and the need to ensure that what happened in the United States of America, and lately in France and Italy, will not be allowed to happen here.'

Outside Parliament there have been many conferences and seminars on the White Paper and its implications. However, most of the effort has been geared towards submissions of evidence to the Home Office, which was requested by 28 February. By then some 3,000 individual submissions had been made.

Subsequent to the debates, three other major events have taken place. The Home Affairs Committee has published a review of the financing of Channel 4; and the Secretary of State has made two statements about the Government's response to the evidence.

On 15 March 1989 the Home Affairs Committee published its report on the financing of Channel 4, in which it recommended:

- Option 2 of the White Paper (Channel 4 as a subsidiary of the ITC) should be adopted;
- Channel 4's funding should be set at a level equivalent to 14 per cent of net advertising revenue;
- the remit should be re-stated in the Bill;
- consideration should be given to amending the arrangements for funding S4C, as the system of levying a first charge on franchise holders could threaten the small companies.

The Home Secretary responded to the report in a letter to the Chairman of the Committee on 13 June. His main points were:

- Option 2 would be the chosen structure, although Channel 4 would become a trust so as to separate its ownership from its regulation;
- funding would be set at 14 per cent of NAR and, should there be a shortfall, the ITC would meet that, through a levy on franchise holders, up to 2 per cent of NAR;
- the remit would be re-stated in the Bill;
- S4C would in future be financed out of the proceeds of the competitive tendering process.

On 19 May, the Home Secretary gave a written statement in which he elaborated the rules governing ownership;

- There would be restrictions on dual ownership to prevent the ownership by one concern of two large or two contiguous franchise areas;
- cross-media ownership would be restricted so that newspaper proprietors could have only up to 20 per cent interest in a television franchise and could not have an interest in more than one franchise.
- non-EC companies would be barred from owning ITC or Radio Authority licences;

- the ITC would be empowered to monitor and control changes in share ownership of the companies.

The Home Secretary made a statement in the House of Commons on 13 June 1989 regarding commercial television. The most significant points were:

- There would be a higher quality threshold for the ITC franchises and the ITC would have power not to award the franchise to the highest bidder 'in exceptional circumstances';
- the levy on Channel 3 companies was to be dropped;
- the Channel 3 franchises were to embrace the night hours, rather than the original proposal to split them into day and night hours;
- Channel 5 was also to be a national franchise.

Subsequently, on 4 July 1989, the Home Secretary made further written statements about the BBC and about the transmission networks:

- The BBC were to retain the night hours on both its channels, rather than just one as originally proposed, provided it maximised the opportunities for subscription revenue afforded by the night hours;
- the transmission networks were to be privatised, but not on the lines suggested in the White Paper of a series of local operators. Instead, the existing BBC and IBA networks were to be retained and sold to two private operators working on a national basis. The BBC would sell its network after 1996; the IBA would sell its network once the Bill was in force. Tariffs would be set at levels reflecting the percentage of total Channel 3 income received by each individual franchise holder. The Director General of Telecommunications would be empowered to regulate the new system to ensure fairness and maintenance of standards.

It might seem that on the basis of these pronouncements, all the major decisions on the White Paper have been taken by the Government. However, there are still many issues to be resolved. Nonetheless, it has become clear that there is no willingness to challenge the

BBC's Royal Charter, and that the Bill, when it comes, will largely deal with the Re-regulation of Commercial Television.

In the following chapters, we have analysed the significant evidence received, in much the same way as a civil servant might have been expected to do for the Ministers concerned. We do not claim to have been comprehensive but, as the list of evidence consulted given in the Appendix shows, most of the key submissions have been utilised.

2
The Government's Approach

General

1. This chapter is a summary of the Government's general approach, underlying all the subsequent specific proposals.

The Government's Aims

2. The Government states in its White Paper that its aims are: to allow individuals 'to choose from a much wider range of programmes'; to introduce a more 'competitive broadcasting market ... without detriment to programme standards and quality'; and to enable broadcasting 'to maintain and strengthen its quality, diversity and popularity' (White Paper, 1.2, p. 1 and 2.2, p. 4). A second aim is to reduce the costs for advertisers of gaining access to large television audiences. The Government's strategy is to dismantle the existing arrangements for regulating commercial television and radio while preserving the BBC and Channel 4 and to allow the market to determine the nature of future broadcasting.

3. The expectation is that, with more channels on the air, individual viewers can exercise greater choice over what they watch and indeed determine the types of programmes actually shown. This is to be achieved either directly, through subscription for example, or indirectly, through an individual's influence over ratings figures. The Government intends to regulate broadcasting in terms of 'decency' but not in terms of the quality of programming in a more general sense. The former standards are regarded by the Government as unsuitable for free market regulation, whereas adequate standards of programmes, it is suggested, can be secured through competition between broadcasters.

The Response

a) *Support for the general approach*

4. A number of submissions prefaced their critique of the White Paper with a general statement about those of its aims which they supported: these were generally the global statements of principle found at the start of the White Paper. The IBA's response was illustrative in this respect of a number of submissions:

> We agree with the assumptions underlying the White Paper that:
>
> The viewer and listener should be placed at the centre of broadcasting policy.
>
> The radical changes which are now likely in the British broadcasting scene require radical changes in the regulatory system and the ways in which broadcasting organisations now operate.
>
> Broadcasting should continue to be independent from Government editorially and, to the greatest possible extent, in economic and regulatory terms.
>
> Quality is appreciated by viewers, as well as choice and competition; we also see a strong indigenous production sector as a basic safeguard for the quality of British television.
>
> The distinctive remit of the fourth channel should be protected.
>
> Subject to clear but limited requirements effectively enforced by the regulator, independent broadcasting organisations should take responsibility for their programmes (including advertisements), operations and decisions.
>
> The aim is to create a flexible framework which allows for social, cultural, technological and market developments in the next ten or fifteen years.
>
> IBA, 1.7, pp. 13–14

b) *Choice and quality*

5. On the key question of choice and quality a very substantial proportion of the evidence reviewed argued that a free market is not a suitable mechanism for ensuring either diversity or quality because it is geared primarily to maximising profits. As a result, the market approach, it was argued, will generally lead to the broadcasting of programmes which stand a good chance of attracting mass

23

audiences. This would point towards a reduction in the present diversity of programmes in favour of a large number of similar, mass appeal programmes designed to secure maximum revenue.

6. Much of the evidence argued that the combination of the Government's proposals to award franchises to the highest bidder, and to exact a levy on the revenue of ITV companies, would exacerbate this tendency, by ensuring that recovery of costs will be of paramount concern to the broadcasters:

> ... the Government's proposals are in danger of losing part of what is best about the current commercial networks. Imposing excessive financial burdens on ITV could lead to the loss of popular, high-quality, British-made fiction and entertainment programmes since these are among the most expensive to produce. There is the further probability that, under the pressure of profit before programme quality, major current affairs and children's programmes and minority interests will all suffer.... The pressure to maximise profits after the auction will be strong.... If the Broadcasting Act enjoins only profit-making on commercial companies, programming will be tailored only to that end. The viewer will be the loser. (ITV, 4.3, p. 15)

7. This conflict between profits and standards is a worldwide phenomenon, which usually resolves itself in favour of one of the two elements, rather than a happy medium:

> If a government could create by decree a group of channels competing commercially without lowering their programme standards ... there would by now exist in one country or another some corroborative historical evidence. None exists. (British Screen Advisory Council, 3.3)

8. The expected increase in choice is unlikely to materialise when a large number of television companies are trying to attract quick profits, as the experience in other countries shows.

> The American system may indeed offer, in numerical terms, more choice; but the choice lies chiefly in fifty slightly different game shows or soap operas – and for the viewer whose tastes run to neither, that is no choice at all. (Scottish Film Council, 2.7, p. 2)

The dawn of the satellite revolution has already proved that more channels do not necessarily mean greater variety ... the economics of satellite production mean that you have to produce 100-plus editions of sit-coms and game shows to make them cost effective. Thus, the viewer will be getting for the foreseeable future such 'revelations' as 'The Price is Right', 'Sale of the Century' and 'I Love Lucy'. Hardly the widening of choice. (British Film and Television Producers Association, 8, p. 12)

Whereas new programmes often need time to build an appreciative audience, tight finances mean that the networks [in the USA] cannot tolerate low ratings performance over a long haul. On several occasions the networks have shown a pattern of trying something a bit different when trying new shows and then cancelling them despite good critical reviews, because initial audiences were lower than hoped. (Prof. Blumler, quoted in ITV, 4.13, p. 18)

9. So the strength of the evidence submitted to the Government suggests that the twin goals of deregulation on the one hand and high quality and diversity on the other are incompatible. Most respondents postulate an environment in which the emphasis is on low-cost, lowest common denominator programming which is likely to maximise audiences. There will be a decline in programme production and an increase in buying in foreign material. Innovation will not be cost-effective and so will not be attempted:

The cost of starting the new services and bidding for the franchises, the lack of regulation and the shrinking revenue that will come from increased competition will all militate against servicing minority tastes, taking risks or applying any other criteria than commercial ones. (Thames TV, quoted in Yorkshire Arts, 3.8, p. 4)

10. But even if standards decline, will the costs of broadcasting at least go down? Many respondents predicted that costs will rise for both broadcasters and advertisers:

Whatever its effect on programmes, competition in broadcasting drives costs up not down.... There will be competition for performers, writers, directors and other scarce resources. The cost of bought-in material will be similarly raised.... More channels will mean more airtime for more advertisers, but the resulting fragmentation of audiences will increase the costs of reaching them, and most advertisers ... will pay more not less. (ITV, 4.18–19, pp. 19–20)

The BBC will continue to improve its ... cost effectiveness; but scope for this will become more limited as ... growing competition in the commercial sector drives up costs, notably for the best drama and films, for major sporting events and for the most talented programme makers and performers. (BBC, 3.4)

11. As a result of the analysis summarised above, a large number of respondents foresaw that the Government's proposals, far from expanding viewer choice, would be likely to reduce it:

There are considerable doubts about whether the cost of new satellite dishes, encrypting equipment for subscription, new aerials etc., will prove attractive to the consumer, especially if they can get higher quality services from the existing duopoly at a lower price. In one sense the rapid attack on the BBC and ITV system in the White Paper is to try and force the consumer into purchasing satellite equipment by destroying or severely undermining the quality of services s/he can currently obtain. This is particularly true of the proposal to privatise transmitters which may have the effect of boosting the demand for satellite dishes simply by removing the terrestrial services in areas such as Wales and Scotland. The Government does not want to repeat the widely recognised debacle of cable where high entry costs discouraged investors and low programme quality put consumers off. To get round the latter the Government seems to be driving the standards of other services down. (Campaign for Press and Broadcasting Freedom, 4.1, p. 15)

... there is no threat to the quality of programmes offered to British viewers through the introduction of new services; there is such a threat if the core Channels are destabilised.

The Government recognises that over the coming years, ten Channels will be available as part of the UK mainstream (5 terrestrial, 5 DBS) together with a number of other Channels delivered via cable or medium power satellite. BSB remains confident that there will be a fast developing market for new services. It is nevertheless unlikely that the majority of people will have acquired the equipment to receive a substantial number of additional Channels before the latter 1990s. Thus the majority, or at least a significant minority, of households will remain dependent on terrestrial Channels until almost the end of the century. It is, therefore, desirable that the range and diversity of programmes on offer through these core services should not be significantly reduced through regulatory changes. It would be ironic if a White Paper which espouses greater choice and places the viewer at the centre of the debate actually leads to a reduction in choice in the medium term for the majority of households. (British Satellite Broadcasting, 8.1–2)

The full numerical choice of channels and stations will not be realisable for those who cannot afford them – the poor, elderly and unemployed – though these are usually those who depend the most on radio and television for information, education, entertainment and company.

In any event, it is a faulty and simplistic argument to suggest, as the White Paper does, that the audience can control programme scheduling by opting daily for the programmes which it prefers.

It is not as though the Government is enabling some pioneering enterprise to take its chances, with no knowledge of the likely outcome. After all, other countries offer a salutary lesson to those who would displace a system in which broadcasting is regulated as a service to the public, with one regulated differently. 'The American system of lighter regulation has resulted in one of the best, most efficient systems ever known for delivering an audience. It has *not* provided and cannot provide a way to satisfy the public's demands.' Stewart Hoover, *The Electronic Giant*, 1982. (Church of England, 19, 21–2)

... in relation to broadcasting, it is far from obvious that the 'market' as such can be relied upon to deliver what consumers want, or that it will optimise the allocation of resources. The links are especially weak in relation to the universally-available commercial services, ITV Channel 3 and Channel 4. Here there is no contract at all between the viewer and the provider of programmes: the contract is between the company and the advertisers. The amount advertisers are willing to pay reflects what they estimate to be the likely popularity of the programmes, but this on its own is no guarantee of programming that will maximise the quality of service the consumer gets from the system as a whole. On the contrary, the advertiser has absolutely no direct interest in the maintenance of a diverse and varied programme schedule of high quality – which we have identified as crucial to the maintenance and promotion of real consumer choice; the advertiser's objective will be met by the most basic programmes possible that will deliver an acceptable level of ratings. With a purely market-led system, there is a real risk of all programmes tending to converge to a single type, which can be guaranteed to command a 'safe' level of ratings, without any risk of cross-subsidy. Yet it is cross-subsidy within the system that effectively promotes variety – a feature found in many other aspects of the media, including book and newspaper publishing.

... the growth of cable and satellite may eventually pose problems for the existing channels, through competition for advertising, for viewers and for key programmes such as sports events. The extent and nature of this threat is as yet unknown; so far it is small, and it may remain small for some years yet. What we find hard to justify is that the universal channels should be sub-stantially reformed *before* the full implications of cable and satel-lite are known, and on the assumption that these will be sweeping.

This reinforces our concern that under the current proposals, viewers who depend solely on the 'universal' tier could lose out compared with what they would have had under the present system – and before any real evidence has been allowed to accumulate that the changes are necessary. We conclude from this that the whole of the 'universal' tier, including Channel 3, will continue to need a substantial measure of regulation, actively to promote diversity, variety and quality – in the interests of main-taining and promoting real consumer choice. (Consumers' Associ-ation, 3.2, 5.5–6, pp. 7–8, 12)

Channel 5 will be on the air in 1993.... It will require a new aerial costing about £50. Satellite channels are being launched this year. The dishes for each are incompatible and could cost about £1000 for viewers to install both.... Subscription to the BSB Movie Channel and the Sky Movies and Disney Channels will cost about £250 a year. It is not yet clear how much viewers might have to pay for the current four channels through subscription and pay per view mechanisms, although it is likely to cost more.... There may indeed be more choice for those who can afford all the new services but for those who wish just to maintain what they have already it will both cost more and be of reduced diversity and quality. The proposals could lead in the direction of a 'television-rich' and a 'television-poor' society. (Yorkshire Arts, 3.12, pp. 4–5)

3
The BBC

The Government's Proposals

1. The Government accept that the BBC's role will be to continue to provide public service broadcasting at a time when the commercial sector is to be de-regulated. Nevertheless, the Government intend to introduce market disciplines into the BBC in two main ways. The first is to phase in subscription as the means of funding the BBC, possibly with a view to replacing the licence fee altogether. The second is to remove the night hours from one of the BBC's channels and sell them to a commercial broadcaster. These changes are not in themselves intended to raise standards, but simply to introduce further elements of market-related broadcasting into the scene.

The Responses

a) *Funding the BBC*

2. The proposal that the BBC should no longer be funded by a licence fee, but should be increasingly a subscription channel, provoked alarm, suspicion, and incomprehension, causing some of those giving evidence to cast doubt on the Government's motives with regard to the BBC:

> Everything in the organising philosophy and proposals of the White Paper points towards the not-so-long-term demolition of the BBC as we now know it. (Centre for Local Economic Strategies, 3.5, p. 25)

3. The responses were virtually unanimous in opposing the move towards subscription. Most respondents have explained that the concept of a national public service broadcasting channel depends upon universal access, regardless of means, and requires adequate public funding to ensure quality programme making. The introduction of subscription would undermine both of these principles:

The reliance on subscription fees for a majority of the BBC's income could only result in a two-tier system of broadcasting – the antithesis of the public service concept. Viewers willing and able to purchase the superior, and more extensive, alternatives would be provided with a service which in many ways is preferable to that which was available to those who did not take advantage of subscription. . . . To allow subscription to become the basic service – with those who cannot afford it relying on a residual general service – totally undermines the concept of public service broadcasting. (Labour Party, pp. 12–13)

. . . the kinds of quality programmes and events that would be most effective in attracting subscribers, such as the Wimbledon Lawn Tennis Championships, will be restricted to those who can afford to pay. Eventually a range of national events which are currently available to everybody, will be available only to subscribers to particular channels. There will be a choice available to those able to pay, at the expense of a diminished choice for the remainder. (Campaign for Quality Television, 8, p. 2)

4. Subscription would not reduce the cost for the viewer:

BBC Television delivers over 200 hours of programmes a week to each household for less than £1. . . . A universal, standard charge makes possible the delivery of a wide range of programming at low cost to the individual, including expensive or special interest output. It broadens the range of material available to everyone. (BBC, 3.2)

There is no evidence that the licence fee is publicly unacceptable. On the contrary, it is rapidly becoming clear just how much of a bargain it is when compared with the costs that members of the public will have to incur if they wish to take advantage of the new non-terrestrial services. (Broadcasting and Entertainment Trades Alliance [BETA], 13, p. 7)

At present, for £62.50 the full range of BBC output is available to 99.9% of the population. The cost is exactly the equivalent of purchasing a daily copy of The Sun newspaper. (Mersey Television Co., 2.4.2, p. 3)

b) *Financing Standards*

5. Doubts were voiced as to whether quality broadcasting could be sustained by subscription:

> Admittedly, a few major sporting events, some entertainment spectaculars and a handful of movies are likely to generate huge sums of pay-per-view cash, but there is no evidence (anywhere in the world) that the direct supply of 'quality' programming will be viable as a subscription base and therefore enable 'public service' broadcasting to survive. (British Film and Television Producers Association, 5, p. 12)

> Any attempt to attract subscribers for current affairs programmes, documentaries, arts programmes or high quality drama would be unlikely to generate enough income to fund those high-cost types of programming. (Campaign for Quality Television, 8, p. 2)

6. If the BBC's support were to be reduced, and the loss to be made up from subscription, it would no longer be in a position to provide high quality, high cost programmes:

> International experience of subscription channels indicates that an average of 70% of airtime is devoted to premium entertainment programming, with minimal information or other public service elements. The BBC, under subscription, would therefore have to drastically alter its programme mix. (Association of Cinematograph, Television and Allied Technicians [ACTT], 69, p. 21)

7. Thus, respondents concluded, the licence fee must remain, fully indexed to the RPI, for the foreseeable future. Most accepted that there was a limited role for subscription in ways such as the BBC's current experimental medical information service.

c) *The Night Hours*

8. There was opposition also to the proposed removal of the night hours from one BBC channel:

> ... to remove one of the BBC channels during night hours would provoke a clash with the occasional night hours coverage (such as for elections or sports events) which viewers rightly expect to continue as a universal service. (ACTT, 71, p. 21)

The proposal ... would reduce both programme flexibility and the commercial opportunity to explore to the full overnight subscription services ... these night hours are not a vital point of entry for new operators. But they are important to the BBC in beginning to develop subscriber services, of a nature only the BBC can offer. (BBC, 4.12)

4
Channel 3

The Government's Proposals

1. The main thrust of the changes proposed by the Government relate to the present ITV system, to be renamed Channel 3. With the BBC retaining a public service remit (although subject to market pressures), the ITV system is to be considerably deregulated to produce a free market broadcasting environment. A licensing body, the ITC, is to replace the present broadcasting authority, the IBA, and will supervise the awarding of franchises and monitor performance thereafter. There will be some basic requirements relating to news and current affairs, to regional production and one or two other factors, but franchise holders will otherwise be free to decide for themselves the type of programming supplied, the way in which programmes are procured and the mix of advertising and subscription. In the White Paper, the system of awarding franchises was to change from the present concentration on the quality of programmes to be supplied to one where, subject to satisfying a minimum quality threshold, the highest bidder would win. Subsequently, the Home Secretary announced that the eventual legislation would introduce a higher quality threshold and that, in exceptional circumstances, the ITC could reject the highest bidder (Hansard, House of Commons, 13 June 1989, cols. 710–13).

2. These proposals reflect the Government's view that, with more channels becoming available through satellite and cable, there is no longer any need to regulate commercial television. The suggestion is that the market will regulate standards, with the viewer exercising choice to determine which channels will survive. Through the imposition of considerable financial burdens on the Channel 3 companies, franchise holders will be induced to compete fiercely for audiences in order to maximise their revenue. In this way, it is proposed, the

33

consumer can be sure of receiving only the best television because the poorer product will be unpopular and thus unable to continue in the market.

The Response

a) *Choice and quality*

3. The evidence sent to the Home Office has pointed out a number of problems with this approach. A preliminary point is that, for some years yet, the vast majority of viewers will still have access only to the existing four terrestrial channels:

> ... we find it difficult to accept the Government's premise that an expanded free market will be the most efficient mechanism for providing consumers with the broadcasting they want. Choice of channels will remain limited for most viewers in the foreseeable future.... Consumers of broadcasting are not able to register their qualitative preferences directly; under these circumstances, we would submit that market forces are inappropriate as the means for fulfilling viewing and listening requirements. (Broadcasting Research Unit, 2.8, p. 3)

> It would be superficial to argue that 'the consumer will choose' as he would in, say, a bookshop because the choice of receiving the services of a rich but mediocre company instead of an efficient and creative company would not be made by the viewer but would be made, in advance, by the ITC. (Television South West, p. 6)

4. A number of submissions expressed doubt about the financial ability or willingness of television companies to provide quality programming under the new arrangements; having had to make a large initial outlay to secure the franchise, their aim is more likely to be to maximise audiences:

> ... the direct effect of auctioning will be a significant cut in programming budgets and a strong incentive for franchisees to narrow the range of programmes, especially during the main viewing hours. (Barwise and Ehrenberg, quoted in ITV, 5.34, p. 38)

> Unless government regulation ensures a sufficiently wide variety of programmes to make choice a reality, the viewers' choice will be limited by the commercial interests of the programme companies. (Labour Party, pp. 2–3).

b) *The auction proposal*

5. The overwhelming weight of opinion was strongly opposed to the auctioning of franchises to the highest bidder. Submission after submission argued that sealed bid auctions, as proposed in the White Paper, would encourage over-bidding to secure the franchise, with the successful bidder then having to reduce expenditure on programmes to a minimum to ensure any profit. This tendency would be reinforced by the levy on revenue, rather than profit, and the minimal standards of programme requirements which can be demanded by the ITC. So, the argument ran, money otherwise available to spend on programmes will be diverted to the Exchequer, and a group of under-resourced television companies will struggle with each other to gain maximum audience ratings from large volumes of the same, largely imported, mediocre populist material. This contrasts with the existing arrangements and their effects:

> One of the strengths of the present structure is that the current ITV/ Channel 4 system is well funded and so has the programme capacity to provide a competitive challenge to the BBC in a way which ensures that quality programming is rewarded. This complex structure is supportable while the monopoly exists in advertising but may be insupportable now that the monopoly is broken ... and if the Government insist on a tender for franchises and a levy on franchise holders' revenue. (British Film Institute [BFI], 1.8, p. 2)

> It is the advertising monopoly which has in the earlier eras of television created the unusual position where a commercial system has produced a large proportion of high quality programmes ... The logic of the White Paper is that ITV, or its substitute, deprived of these resources, will pursue minimal rather than maximal objectives and jettison the good things formerly affordable. Could this be to anyone's benefit? (British Screen Advisory Council, 5.9, p. 13)

6. There was little doubt expressed about what the new regime would bring:

> Given that C3 companies will have large 'market entry' fees to pay off, and minimal programming obligations, the effects on programme diversity are obvious. . . . [the new system] has to be one

built on continuous audience maximisation: a much narrower, coarser version of ITV, shorn of anything but the most token vestiges of programme breadth and diversity. (Centre for Local Economic Strategies, 3.2, p. 20)

Most advertisers and viewers who have carefully considered the consequences of the Government's proposals believe that programme standards will fall. Licensees would in practice be able to narrow the range of programmes more under a regime which emphasised the financial bid than one which emphasised the range and quality of programmes. One cannot simultaneously maximise both. (ITV, 5.41.4, pp. 42–3)

We find it hard to accept that a system which has encouraged investment in better programmes and quality productions should be replaced by one which merely guarantees a return to the Treasury.... Companies tempted to overbid to secure a franchise will be seeking to repay their debt in the shortest possible time. Inexpensive programming, with the maximum number of imports, will be the fastest means of turning loss into profit. The object of the Government's proposals – securing the best deal for viewers and listeners will be utterly undermined. (Broadcasting Research Unit, 3.8, 3.11, pp. 6–7)

There can be little doubt that if the new licensees have to pay through the nose for their licences, they will look to the cheapest programmes compatible with mass audiences – often bought in from overseas. We don't want to see high quality arts programmes squeezed out by mass audience programming designed to capture mass audience advertising. (National Campaign for the Arts)

7. The IBA, in its submission, attempted to set out the way in which the Government's auction proposals would need to operate if the viewer were to receive an adequate service. The IBA first drew attention to the importance of securing a diverse programme service from applicants for franchises:

The interpretation of the requirement for 'a diverse programme service calculated to appeal to a wide variety of tastes and interests' will, above all else, determine the character of Channels 3 and 5. Popular entertainment, such as quizzes and soaps, is bound to feature prominently, but more original and challenging drama and comedy programmes which are highly valued by viewers but expensive to produce should not be squeezed out of peak time. We assume that the ITC will consider including requirements for other kinds of programming, for instance children's programming or religious or arts programming in the licences it will advertise for Channels 3 and 5. (IBA, 4.30, p. 29)

8. The IBA submission then went on to argue that, if such proposals for quality programming were to be translated into an actual service, then the auction process had to ensure that the successful bidders were able to meet their obligations:

However, viewers will suffer if licensees are not able to deliver the services which they undertake to provide. Given the economic pressures likely to be felt in the 1990s, sanctions in support of quality requirements will achieve little if the licensee does not have the capabilities and resources to support a service to the required standard for the duration of the licence. We consider that a successful selection process for licensees cannot depend solely on the highest bid, but must also entail a judgment by the ITC as to the relative soundness and durability of financial plans, of which the bid is a part. (IBA, 5.5, p. 36).

9. As a result, the financial soundness of a bidder *and* the quality of service proposed would have to be considered *at the same time*, and not in the two separate stages advocated by the White Paper:

For the reasons given, we regard it as essential that assessment of the quality requirements and the tender should be treated not as separate and successive stages, but as unified parts of a single process. The need to assess the capability of applicants to generate sufficient revenue to support all obligations in the licence means that the bid must be taken into account when the soundness of the applicant's business plan as a whole is assessed. [...] Particular emphasis would be laid on assessing the 'quality' of each applicant's money, the realism of the expected income streams from the programme proposals, the likelihood of securing the programming and the way in which resources so generated would be used within the applicant company to meet each requirement of the licence. Assessment should be concentrated on the first five years of the licence term when plans and economic circumstances were more certain. But the framework of assessment would be the full term. The central question would be whether undertakings made, including the bid, were financially sustainable. (IBA, 5.16, 5.20, pp. 39–40)

10. Advertisers shared the general concern about the future quality of programmes:

... whatever system is finally adopted for the awarding of franchises, it should be one which recognises the overriding objective to ensure a rich and diverse programme service of high quality. (Institute of Practitioners in Advertising, p. 7)

c) *Regulating standards*

11. Concern that the ITC, as a mere licensing body, would not be able to ensure standards of programming led a number of respondents to advocate far more detailed programme requirements, ability to satisfy which should determine the awarding of franchises:

... virtually the only strand of television programming to receive constant attention in the White Paper with regard to the necessity of quality is news and current affairs. This may justifiably reflect the priorities of politicians as viewers and consumers. But it is regrettable that the White Paper does not take any opportunity to make the same emphasis with reference to drama, light entertainment, children's programmes, multi-cultural programmes, sport, arts programming and all the other strands which give British Broadcasting its well-deserved international reputation. Important as news and current affairs are, there are many programmes which are watched by even more of the viewers whom the Government purports to place at the centre of its policies. (Scottish Film Council, 3.4.2, p. 6)

There is no doubt that the range and proportion of high quality programming on ITV has been a direct result of the obligations imposed by the IBA. If the ITC's positive programme requirements for Channels 3 and 5 are weaker than the IBA's existing requirements for ITV, the increase in the number of programmes transmitted will be accompanied by a reduction in the range, quality and diversity of programmes available. What quality there is on ITV has stemmed from obligation, rather than market forces or the simple pursuit of profit. (Campaign for Quality Television, 17, p. 4)

d) *The auction and competition*

12. It was further put in some submissions that the highest-bidder-wins system was anti-competitive:

> ... the barriers to entry would be raised to an impossible level. The right to operate an ITV station would become the exclusive preserve of those with the deepest pockets.... The giants would be able to keep all but the most powerful newcomers out. (Television South West, p. 6)

> ... the system is unfair because it permits those with greater resources to outbid better broadcasters.... (Dr Veljanovski, quoted in ITV, 5.42, p. 44)

> Competitive tendering favours large, established companies with substantial cash reserves and acts as a disincentive to new smaller entrants. (National Union of Journalists, 19, p. 7)

e) *The levy*

13. The original proposal in the White Paper was to supplement the auction with a levy on revenue; subsequently, the Home Secretary announced that the Government were to drop the levy and to fix the franchise prices as a lump sum plus a percentage of net advertising revenue. This followed much criticism of the original proposal, with many respondents suggesting that there was no longer any justification for a levy:

> The levy was introduced ... in recognition of the monopoly which the stations had on television advertising revenue. This monopoly no longer exists and it is clearly unfair to continue to apply levy in an open market where franchises are already paid for – an open market where other channels are not singled out for such treatment. (Grampian Television, 3.9, p. 22)

> The ISBA and other advertisers are particularly opposed to the levy ... in the form of a percentage of advertising revenue. We believe that this will have the unfortunate effect of causing advertising costs to rise even higher, and imposing further pressure on the programme budgets of each licence-holder, where we want to see good quality programmes encouraged. We urge the Government to do away with the whole proposal for a levy from 1993 onwards. (Incorporated Society of British Advertisers, 3, p. 2)

f) Regional production

14. Further deleterious consequences of the Government's proposals for ITV were identified in respect of regional production:

> An important aspect of ITV's regionalism is the dispersal of major production centres throughout the country. Not only are programmes made for 18 individual regions by ITV companies; programmes are also made in production centres throughout the UK for national transmission. Thus Britain broadcasts to Britain, in contrast to the market forces answer which could well lead to London broadcasting to Britain. (ITV, 7.4, p. 58)

15. Under the Government's proposals, a different outcome was predicted:

> There are grave dangers that deregulation will lead to a greater concentration of ownership with a handful of London-based or transnational companies dominating the market. Our concern is that both the freelance sector and the in-house regional centres of the BBC and ITV will suffer ... with considerable consequences for indigenous creativity and cultural production. (Yorkshire Arts, 4.10, p. 7)

> It requires less effort and probably less expense for regional ITV companies to work entirely through London independents, allowing the regional production capacity to wither. (Yorkshire Television, 5, p. 6)

> The effect of current proposals will be to force smaller, less viable regions to amalgamate with larger neighbouring regions, thereby losing any distinctive appeal. This will be the effect of the 'market' solution which will not take account of the disparate economic conditions in different parts of the country: the greater economic wealth of the South will enable it to sustain more regional stations than the North, regardless of local demands. (Broadcasting Research Unit, 3.15, p. 7)

> Without a strengthened and explicit requirement for regional production, there is a strong danger that all but a rump of regional news production may gravitate towards London. This would be undesirable, not just for regionally-based programme-makers but for the whole economic and cultural life of the regions. It is a

valuable characteristic of the UK television industry that so much production is not metropolitan in origin and is in fact dispersed throughout the country. Not only is there a valuable regional dimension of input into British broadcasting, but the very presence of production facilities and skills contributes significantly to the economic and cultural life of the regions/nations within the UK. Without a positive requirement to maintain this, it is easy to foresee the development of a UK broadcasting industry which is overwhelmingly metropolitan. (ACTT, 41, p. 14)

g) *Networking*

15. The IBA stressed the importance of preserving the present network arrangements in the new Channel 3 if competition with the BBC were to be maintained:

Networking of programmes means each region showing the same programme (normally at the same time) as every other region for an agreed number of hours. It has the following advantages:

High quality programmes will be made if the broadcasters can afford to pay for them, and their ability to pay will depend upon the size of the audience. A single network allows the costs of programmes to be spread amongst all the companies, thereby minimising their costs at a time when resources are likely to be constrained.

A network schedule gives simultaneous national exposure to major events, performers and writers. This is very important in competing for talent with other networks both terrestrial and satellite.

A network schedule enables Channel 3 to provide a strong and necessary competition for the BBC and other services and a basis for complementarity with Channel 4.

A network schedule provides the spine supporting regional interest programmes. It is also the means by which regional programmes are seen by viewers throughout the UK – 'showing Britain to the British'.

A network schedule provides a continuity and diversity of programmes which is crucial in building and holding audiences.

A network schedule is attractive to advertisers. Since it enables the commercial sector to compete more successfully against the BBC, it reduces cost per thousand.

41

The current choice and competition between independent television and the BBC should be maintained. If the third principle of the White Paper – quality – is also to be maintained, networking on Channel 3 is essential. We do not believe that a network would necessarily be created without the support of legislation or a licence requirement. If such provision is not made, the commercial uncertainty could distort the outcome of competitive tendering for Channel 3 and prevent the true price of a licence emerging at the outset. The Government should enable the ITC to require a network and to approve the arrangements for it. The network should be run on competitive principles. (IBA, 4.34–5, p. 30)

h) *The number of regions*

16. A further specific point to which many submissions drew attention was the suggestion in the White Paper that the ITC should reconsider the number of regions for commercial television. Responses from a range of organisations opposed the creation of 'mega regions' as detracting from the genuinely regional nature of a television service. Some advertisers, however, preferred the prospect of macro regions as liable to be more attractive for advertisers wishing to reach larger audiences, with arrangements for localised programming within the mega regional structure. Typical responses from those opposing the larger regions were are follows:

We believe that the creation of 'mega regions' by joining together existing separate franchises would be a very unfortunate development. It is viewers, not advertisers, who are the most important constituency, and they would clearly lose if ITV stations were to become more remote and less rooted in the existing franchise areas. Some of these regions are already very large and some companies (e.g. Central) have therefore moved in precisely the opposite direction by establishing new sub-regional services. In our view this should be supported and maintained. (ACTT, 29, p. 12)

A 'macro region' would be too large for genuinely regional programming and too small for national programming, and it would reduce to an unacceptable degree the market for independent programme makers, advertisers and employees.

Local 'opt outs' or 'split transmissions' are not the answer as they are disruptive to scheduling, they present formidable engineering problems and they are a mere appendage to the mainstream business of the company. They are accordingly no substitute for genuine regional broadcasting. There would be little or no benefit to the public from economies of scale and experience shows that it is the larger, not the smaller, ITV companies which have suffered most from overmanning and restrictive practices.

A particular advantage of relatively small regions to the advertiser is that the small local business can have access to television advertising, and can thereby achieve substantial increases in its customer-base. The rates charged by a national or macro regional station would be much too high and the catchment area too large for such businesses. (Television South West, pp. 11–12)

GLA believes that the existing number of franchise-holders for Channel 3 should be maintained. A reduction is likely adversely to affect regional coverage by providing less opportunity for geographically focussed programming, and fewer franchises would also reduce the likelihood of diverse programming. (Greater London Arts, 3.2, p. 2)

17. The other side of the argument was, numerically, far less represented, but two examples follow:

The IPA stands by its earlier proposal that the boundaries for the new Channel 3 franchises be redrawn into six 'macro regions' (plus Ulster). However, we would like to emphasise that, in our earlier proposal, we stated that this realignment of franchise boundaries would in no way preclude a new franchise holder meeting local programming (and advertising) demand by use of split transmission facilities within the macro region. (Institute of Practitioners in Advertising, p. 6)

We believe that the present 15-company federal system under which ITV operates is costly, unwieldy and inefficient. It is impossible to run such a system in a brisk and efficient manner. It is doubtful if such a system can be commercially sustainable in the more competitive nineties. . . .

The economic viability of small licence areas is doubtful now and will become increasingly so. The provision of a first-class service to regions can be supplied by the licence holder of larger areas. There are, for example, three dual franchise areas in existence and we have recently launched a third dedicated news and advertising service known as Central South. There is little doubt that resources expended on the infrastructure of the 15-company system could be released to devote more money to a stronger and more effective regional programming service. (Central TV, 4.1–2)

i) Separation of the night-hours franchise

18. The Government's original proposal was to split franchises into day-time and night-hours operations. This was another proposal on which the Government subsequently changed its view, the Home Secretary announcing in June that the night hours would not be split off from the day-time franchises. This followed submissions from various bodies (mainly the TV companies), which argued that such a separation would place the regional commercial channels at a disadvantage compared to the 24-hour broadcasting ability of all other channels, and would be needlessly inefficient in its duplication of costs and overheads. Those in favour (the advertisers) saw opportunities for additional competition in the selling of advertising time through the increase in the number of companies providing services:

> The night-time hours should not be offered as a separate franchise. In common with all ITV companies, Grampian has pioneered this extension of service to viewers, investing in its gestation period and building regional audiences. Thanks to our automation and use of existing facilities, we can maintain a viable night time service.
> This would not be possible as a separate franchise and so we will see another loss of regional service with the night hours becoming a national licence. This would take further revenue away from regional licences and deprive local audiences and advertisers. . . .
> Contrary to the policy of dispersing jobs from the London area, more national channels will have the effect of moving employment to the South along with more advertising revenue as national advertisers make bookings with a single network channel rather than separately with the regions. (Grampian TV, 3.8, p. 21)

ITV has already lost the hours between 6.30 am and 9.30 am to a breakfast-time contractor. It would be regrettable if the only nationwide service organised on a regional basis were to be reduced to a 16-hour broadcasting day, punctuated by services which were entirely different in character and structure. (Scottish Television, p. 7)

The ITC will have to evaluate carefully whether further subdivision of the Channel 3 service by the separation of the night-time hours and the division of the Channel 5 service will help to achieve [effective use of advertising revenue]. The more the market is fragmented, the more likely it is that each individual independent television service will have insufficient funds to provide the standard and range of programmes which viewers value, and to which they have become accustomed. Fragmentation carries with it a greater risk that quality will be eroded as financially straitened services are forced to broadcast increasing amounts of acquired and imported material....

The night-time services developed in the last year by the ITV companies are a significant part of the service they offer, both in network and regional terms. To fragment the Channel 3 clock by allocating a separate night-time service would constrict the service provided by the licencees at the end of the evening. A stand-alone night-time service would be unlikely to generate sufficient revenue either to provide a reasonable service or provide a significant return to the Treasury. (IBA, 2.13, 4.9, pp. 19, 24)

Practical experience of night-hours' broadcasting by most ITV companies has demonstrated that a separate licence could not be viable, except *possibly* if no original production were undertaken. The prospects for *multiple* night-time licences would seem even more remote.

This is why many ITV companies use the night hours to cater to special-interest groups on a regional basis. The night hours also offer opportunities for new or small regional advertisers. Both these benefits would be denied under a national franchise for the night hours and would not be available from any other channel.

In order to be viable, therefore, any night-time contractor would have to obtain dispensation from the independent production quota (as has occurred with TV–am), or any EEC and/or Council of Europe Convention provisions on European production. Any such dispensation would be inequitable to other licensees....

The division of channel time into day-parts is unique to the UK and it appears to run counter to the Government's desire for greater efficiency in the television industry. Surely, the duplication of costs (overheads, airtime sales, presentation, production, acquisition of programming and separate transmission) across a number of very

45

small broadcasters will not create an efficient broadcasting industry, but rather the opposite. We also believe that the division of Channel Five into day-parts will reduce revenue to the Treasury and significantly increase the commercial risk undertaken by Channel Five contractor(s). (TVS Television Ltd., p. 23)

We welcome the proposal for separate night-time franchises on Channel 3, and on one of the BBC wavelengths, but we would urge the Government and the ITC to reconsider the hours that are given to the licence holders for night-time broadcasting. The very short time span suggested by the Peacock Committee (1 a.m. to 6 a.m.) would make it extremely difficult for a contractor to operate a viable and profitable service, and we urge that the timetable is set out somewhat differently. We would like to see night-time franchises begin at 11 p.m. and certainly before midnight. (Incorporated Society of British Advertisers, p. 4)

j) *Children's television*

19. We have already reviewed the weight of evidence which argued for more comprehensive positive programme requirements to be imposed on franchise holders. Some submissions focused on drama, others on religious broadcasting, still others on sport and so on; but the omission in the White Paper which seemed most surprising was that of children's television:

At present, television for children is concentrated in the early evening on weekdays and in the mornings at weekends. Both BBC and ITV provide programmes which attempt to maintain a diversity in form and content: short animation films and games are mixed with live action drama, current affairs and activity programmes like *Playbus* and *Blue Peter*. Though not uncritical, parents value the attention which television pays to the needs of children, especially those below eight years. Both channels resist the temptation to start building the mass family audiences through scheduling soap operas or game shows very early in the evening. There is a degree of choice and competition about children's programmes at the present time which serves the consumers reasonably well, and which has, indeed, produced quality programmes. . . .

[Deregulation] is unlikely to lead to the production of programmes of high quality. Quality programmes, as the independent television companies freely admit, are not economical to produce

46

and result in a net loss. The companies only continue to provide good programmes for children because the IBA obliges them to do so in order to retain their franchise. In the absence of a similar regulatory body, it is unlikely that anything other than programmes bought in at low cost from abroad will be available on the independent channels. (British Action for Children's Television, 6.5, 6.7, pp. 5, 6)

The Writers' Guild feels that the absence of references in the White Paper to children's television (as opposed to schools television) can only be an oversight on the part of the Government, which is surely aware of and sympathetic to the needs of our children....

In an age when family values are constantly under threat, it is essential to guarantee that the nine million British children currently viewing receive on British television their own life-enhancing diet of homegrown drama, features, light entertainment and information, available at the traditional post-school transmission time. This requires special funding, since high quality in children's programmes costs no less than high quality in programmes made for adults. (Writers' Guild)

We would like to suggest that children's programmes also become a statutory requirement. At present this type of programming is under threat in ITV – Channel 4 having already cancelled its commitment – yet we consider such programming as equally important as News and Current Affairs.

It is slightly ironic that much of the 'taste, decency and impartiality arguments' put forward to support the BSC, BCC and many of the provisions of the White Paper itself endorse the need to protect children. They need not only protection – but stimulation – in a form and content they can understand and accept. (Mersey Television Co., 6.11, p. 14)

k) *Educational television*

20. Schools broadcasting and adult education was another issue raised in some submissions:

The proposed ITC is required to 'plan for and arrange *adequate* provision of schools broadcasts' but there is a complete lack of definition over what is deemed adequate and how and when such broadcasts are to be delivered. At present there is a requirement to provide a *comprehensive* schools broadcasting service. Accordingly, schools programmes will be at risk with the change from 'comprehensive' to 'adequate' opening up a 'channel of avoidance'. (National Association of Head Teachers, (e), p. 2)

The proposals in the White Paper make no stipulation as to how the schools services will be offered; night-time transmission or satellite would seem to be possibilities. At present, however, the very high take-up of programmes (96% of primary schools use schools broadcasts, for example) is related to their availability in school hours. Few schools have more than one video recorder and many primary schools have none. If the BBC and the commercial channels reschedule schools programmes in order to make more competitive use of daytime transmission, their accessibility to consumers will be seriously impaired. . . .

Aside from these uncertainties, it should be noted that broadcasting in the nineties could have an important part to play in helping to deliver many aspects of the National Curriculum. The Foundation Subjects of the curriculum already provide the basis of many schools programmes; various subject committees are now defining more specifically what is to be taught and how, and methods of assessment are being developed. By 1990 most of this work will be complete, and television and radio could have a clear and central role both in delivering the National Curriculum in the classroom and in providing in-service support for teachers who will be responsible for this task. An alignment of the aims and objectives of the new curricula within the National Curriculum and the schools programmes provided by radio and television would be a coherent educational enterprise where the resources of the BBC and the independent companies more closely complement national educational provision. For adults, radio and television could have a useful role in offering to parents the knowledge that would enable them to make best use of the opportunities opened up to them by the Education Reform Act. (British Action for Children's Television, 4.1, 5.4, pp. 2, 3)

l) *Media education*

21. A related issue was that of media education, both at schools and via educational broadcasting:

The White Paper acknowledges 'the unique power of the broadcasting media to shape perceptions, and their influence over atti-

48

tudes and actions' (Paragraph 7.2). Given that this power is almost certain to increase in the next decade, there is the strongest case for encouraging education about the media at all levels from the primary school to the adult education class. The broadcast media themselves are well placed to foster this development, along with agencies like the National Curriculum Council and the BFI. (British Action for Children's Television, 5.5, p. 4)

The White Paper's proposals could offer opportunities for television forms and vocabularies to grow rapidly and to encourage new economies and cultures of viewing and production. But crucial to these potential changes is the need to make increased air time and access by independent producers a genuine forum for research, growth and innovation. The role of media education in supporting new producers with knowledge and practices needs to be recognised and developed. Media education concerned with the understanding of form and familiarisation of television practices can build a genuinely televisually literate society in the 1990s and act as a spur to innovation in the medium. (Sussex University Broadcasting Study Group, 6.2, p. 7)

5
Channel 5

The Government's Proposals

1. The Government propose to establish a new Channel 5 from 1993. It will be a national service, and the original proposal for separate franchises for daytime and for the night hours was subsequently dropped. The franchise will be awarded by the ITC on the same basis as for Channel 3; the franchise holder will be free to decide the mix of advertising and subscription and the same 'light touch' regulatory regime will apply, leaving the television company to set its own programme standards, in consultation with the ITC. The intentions here are 1) to increase viewer choice through an additional channel – although it will only be available to about 70 per cent of the population and will require a new aerial; and 2) to 'bring significant relief to the advertising market' (White Paper, 6.21, p. 24)

The Response

2. Responses focused on a limited number of issues: the standard of programmes which should be offered by the new channel; its location; and the likely effects on advertising costs.

a) *Programme standards*

3. As Channel 5 will be a completely new, national terrestrial channel, the Government can have a significant influence over the nature of its programme regime. There was a wide consensus that it should aim to provide the sort of high quality broadcasting already established in parts of British television and to cater for any gaps left in the new broadcasting environment:

> As there may be gaps in provision after the White Paper is implemented, the following programme strands [for Channel 5] should

be given priority when the franchise applications are considered:
- Open University and Open College programmes
- children's programmes
- young people's programmes
- an Arts channel
- parliamentary programmes
- documentary programmes. (BFI, 3.14, p. 14)

By competing with ITV on a narrower revenue base and with no distinctive programming remit, the end result is likely to be a channel that offers little scope for original production and is forced to rely on a large amount of acquired programming. Neither viewers nor programme makers would gain significantly. ... For Channel Five to enhance our broadcasting system ... a strong programming remit is required. (ACTT, 82–3, p. 24)

4. Advertisers themselves supported this approach:

... we hope that the decision of the licence holders will be for programmes which may attract more support of commercial television in total by competing with BBC schedules rather than competing directly with Channel 3. On Channel 5, it will be important for the programmes to be clearly differentiated from the two existing commercial channels so that Channel 5 takes on a character of its own. (Incorporated Society of British Advertisers, 5, p. 4)

5. The IBA suggested that Channel 5 should complement Channel 3's public service role:

Some of the programmes on Channel 3 will not attract large audiences and the channel's revenue prospects will be constrained. As currently envisaged, Channel 5 will not face these constraints. We believe that positive programme requirements should be shared between Channels 3 and 5 so as to provide for fairer and more balanced competition. (IBA, 2.8, p. 18)

b) *The location of Channel 5*

6. Many of those who commented on Channel 5 argued for it to be located outside the South-East:

Channel 5 should have a different character to other services ... the decision to base a broadcasting organisation in a particular location has a profound effect on the local economy and provides a significant boost to local cultural development. We would therefore recommend that Channel 5's headquarters be based outside London and the South-East. (Independent Programme Producers Association, 5.1, p. 8)

c) *The effect on advertising costs*

7. The likelihood of Channel 5 securing 'relief' for advertisers was questioned by a number of respondents, who envisaged advertising costs rising under the new regime. Those who would suffer accordingly were not, however, the advertisers:

It is a common fallacy to believe that advertisers pay for the ITV system.... It is the purchasers of those products whose price includes advertising expenses who pay for ITV. (Sussex University Broadcasting Study Group, 3.4, pp. 3–4)

[The White Paper] seeks to send advertising costs down but it is liable in practice to cause them to rise even higher, since an advertiser will need to buy far more slots of time to reach the same proportion of the population as in the past, or will be forced to pay far more than now for any slots of advertising time which are known still to command very large audiences.... ultimately of course the consumer will face the bill for the increased cost of advertising. (British Screen Advisory Council, 6.4, p. 15)

... the wisdom of creating another channel to be financed out of advertising revenue must, we think, be questioned ... established brand leaders advertise to ensure continued market prominence rather than specifically to increase sales. If a new advertising medium becomes available, such manufacturers will feel it necessary to buy appropriate advertising space in addition to their present advertising expenditure. It is quite possible that the consequent rise in manufacturers' overall costs will be passed on to the purchaser. (Scottish Film Council, 3.3.7, p. 5)

6
Channel 4

The Government's Proposals

1. The Government wish to see Channel 4 continue to provide a public service style of broadcasting to compete with the BBC. It thus remains committed to preserving Channel 4's distinctive remit. Nevertheless, the White Paper argues that the changes to the commercial sector will make the current arrangements for C4 untenable. Further, the Government have accepted the advertisers' wishes for competition in the selling of air time and thus propose that C4 should assume responsibility for its own advertising sales. Three options for changing C4's structure were proposed in the White Paper, including full privatisation or becoming a non-profit-making subsidiary of the ITC. While this latter option (option 2 in the White Paper) would provide a guaranteed income for C4, to ensure the preservation of the remit, the White Paper went on to argue that any such support might lead to 'sterile elitism and precious self-indulgence'.

2. The Government thus appear to be suspicious of the remit while simultaneously seeking to preserve it, and determined to alter the arrangements which have sustained the remit while hoping that this will not adversely affect it. This was a part of the White Paper where the Government seemed genuinely unsure or divided over what the overall aim should be. In the event, the Home Secretary announced in June that C4 would operate within its present remit as a public trust, selling its own advertising and subject to a baseline budget of 14 per cent of net advertising revenue. The baseline would be guaranteed up to 2 per cent of NAR by a levy on the commercial companies.

3. The White Paper acknowledged that S4C cannot live off sales of advertising in its own region and it was thus proposed to continue the present subsidy levied on the ITV companies. The final proposal is

to fund S4C from the revenues raised by the franchise auctions. The remit of S4C, too, is to be preserved.

The Response

4. With the possible exception of the proposals regarding franchise auctions, this part of the White Paper provoked more alarm and hostility than any other. Broadly speaking, advertisers argued that C4 should become financially self-sufficient, while just about everyone else concluded that the remit was not sustainable unless C4 had a guaranteed level of support. The overwhelming weight of opinion argued against C4 competing for advertising revenue with Channel 3 and supported the existing arrangements, accepting option 2 if the changes were insisted upon. (No submission expressed fears about elitism or self-indulgence.)

a) *Channel 4's remit*

5. It is a somewhat arbitrary procedure to select illustrative quotes in this matter as so many submissions spoke with the same voice:

> The most popular programmes on Channel 4 would fit naturally into both the BBC and ITV schedules – the specialist and minority programmes would not. Any attempt by Channel 4 to compete directly for mass advertising revenue would lead to a shift in the balance between these two kinds of programme and Channel 4's unique contribution to the broadcasting mix would be lost. (Campaign for Quality Television, 37, p. 7)

> The success of Channel 4 stems entirely from its protected status within the IBA system. Because it has not been forced to compete for high-rating audiences, it has had the freedom to pursue original ideas and satisfy the programming needs of minority groups previously unfulfilled. This remit cannot be sustained if Channel 4 is forced to compete for audiences with Channel 3 and other commercial channels. (Broadcasting Research Unit, 3.19, pp. 8–9)

> The separation of Channel 4 from its present financing arrangements is likely to affect its remit. We do not believe that the case for moving away from the status quo is convincing. If Channel 4 has to sell its own advertising, we believe that the ITC should be given the duty of guaranteeing Channel 4's income. We feel this could

most easily be achieved by leaving the financing base for Channel 4 as a function of all the other advertising-financed channels, with a guaranteed minimum level agreed in perpetuity. (BFI, 3.18, p. 15)

We urge the Government to let Channel Four remain a company without individual shareholders, and without the obligation to raise its entire revenue in competition with Channel Three, but rather to draw its income under the aegis of the ITC possibly as a negotiated proportion of the total advertising revenue of other commercial channels. Channel Four could thus retain its 'innovative' remit and its airtime could be sold in whole or in part by the companies constituting Channels Three and Five. (British Screen Advisory Council, p. 18)

b) *The advertisers' case*

6. The advertisers pressed the case for C4 to sell its own advertising, but expressed their concern for the preservation of the remit:

Advertisers wish to see the present Channel 4 remit safeguarded because it provides them with the opportunity to reach viewing groups in a more selective way, and therefore a more cost-effective way, than is possible with ITV. (Institute of Practitioners in Advertising, p. 1)

We believe that commercial television, just as much as the BBC, should cater for all tastes and sections of the population, which it has clearly failed to do in recent years. We see Channel Four as playing a very important part in redressing this balance in the future, and we would like to repeat our view that the demand from advertisers and viewers will be for more 'quality' programming which stimulates the imagination, not for less. (Incorporated Society of British Advertisers, supplementary memorandum 1, p. 2)

7. These bodies also proposed arrangements for 'safety net' loans or funding to support C4's remit, should its own income from advertising sales prove insufficient. Their emphasis, however, was on the separation of C4 from Channel 3.

c) *Channel 4's case*

8. Channel 4 itself felt that it *could* survive through selling its own advertising, but that its remit would in certain respects be diluted:

There is a small number of programmes on Channel 4 (for example American Football, and the youth music programme Wired) which do attract a premium. Income from these programmes, which represent only a small part of the range of the schedule, can never on their own compensate commercially for the effects of the comparative smallness of the Channel's overall audience share. Many of the 'special interest' subjects which contribute to the diversity of the magazine market – fishing, parliamentary coverage or ethnic interests for example – are unlikely to support a high level of advertising expenditure on television. Not only is television advertising considerably more expensive to buy but also 'specialist' television programmes fail to deliver sufficiently segmented audiences. . . .

Chasing premium income would certainly entail losing less advertiser-attractive output (for example education, religion and programmes for the handicapped). In any event we are highly sceptical that such a policy would deliver the promised extra income. In pursuing this course the Channel would cease to address important sections of its present audience. The remit would thus be distorted to meet the needs of advertisers, rather than the interests of *all* viewers – with a consequential narrowing of choice.

In summary, we feel that separate selling is viable, but that there is a real danger that advertising interests will exert pressure to exploit certain parts of the Channel's output, whilst abandoning the rest. Great care must be taken to avoid precisely those dangers of weakening the remit, which the White Paper is anxious to avoid. (Channel 4, 3.9, 3.11–12, p. 8)

d) *The ITV companies' case*

9. The ITV companies largely shared the view that a competing C4 was not desirable; however, if C4 was to separate, then existing arrangements for complementary scheduling and cross-promotion should cease:

We continue to search for a solution to the Channel 4 conundrum based on the Government's principal objective of maintaining C4's remit, while separating its sales force and financing from ITV, and subjecting it to market disciplines. Regrettably, we find these objectives incompatible. We should point out that if ITV is separated from C4 the separation should, in our view, be total, leaving ITV and C4 free to compete. (Central TV, 7.1)

56

Yorkshire Television believes that there is no halfway house in relation to the Channel 4 debate. If the maintenance of the Channel 4 remit is of ultimate importance, it seems clear that the current situation achieves this requirement. The alternative to maintaining the status quo, if that is politically difficult to sustain, would be, we recommend, a complete separation in all respects of Channel 4 from Channel 3. Advertisers and their agencies have categorically stated that Channel 4 would be able to maintain its remit on the revenue that it would generate, within the normal competitive processes of a free market. (Yorkshire Television, 6, p. 7)

If the Government values Channel Four's remit to the extent stated in the White Paper, TVS believes that it will be necessary to retain the present arrangements for Channel Four. . . .

If the present arrangements (or some modifications) are not retained, TVS recommend that there should be no legislated links of any nature between Channel Three and Channel Four. (TVS Television, 6, p. 27)

e) *S4C and Gaelic programmes*

10. There was general support for the proposals regarding S4C, and suggestions that they might be duplicated for other regions:

It is clear that many direct benefits have accrued to the Welsh media industries and to cultural activity in Wales from the establishment of S4C in Cardiff. It prompts the question of whether such benefits might flow if the other national regions had similar arrangements with Channel 4, although not necessarily predicated on a language base, and we recommend that considerations should be given to setting up such Channels. (BFI, 3.17, p. 14)

11. However, there was at least one dissenting voice over the future arrangements for S4C:

We applaud S4C's success in achieving its remit. However, we question whether in the more competitive situation in the later half of the 1990s such support for the 500,000 or so Welsh speaking viewers to whom S4C is primarily directed can continue to be provided from within the independent broadcasting system. We are also aware of pressures from other parts of the UK to provide more programming in other languages. (IBA, 4.23, p. 27)

12. The Scottish Film Council was one of a number of voices calling for a more general view of Gaelic-language broadcasting (a request seemingly accepted by the Home Secretary in his June announcement):

The contrast with provision for Welsh speakers via S4C is remarkable, since as Commun na Gaidhlig has pointed out, the Government's own figures demonstrate that audiences for Gaelic programmes such as BBC Scotland's *Prosbaig* exceed many of those for S4C, despite the fact that there are considerably more Welsh than Gaelic speakers.

This is an area which requires much more thought from the Government than it has received, virtually in parenthesis, in the White Paper. The Scottish Office should, we believe, make special and urgent provision for meeting the demand for more programmes in Gaelic. (SFC, 3.10. 2–3, p. 9)

7
Ownership

The Government's Proposals

1. The Government propose to draw up rules to restrict concentration of ownership following the deregulation of broadcasting. At the same time, it intends to reduce the powers of the IBA/ITC to restrict takeovers. This reflects the Government's attempt to strike a balance in this area. On the one hand, the Government recognise that, under the new arrangements, large corporations will be able to control broadcasting in a monopolistic fashion through their greater financial power. On the other hand, the Government wish to limit the ITC's regulatory role which might otherwise have prevented uncompetitive practices arising.

The Response

2. The evidence wholeheartedly endorsed the attempt to limit concentration of ownership and cross-media ownership, but usually argued for tighter restrictions than the Government appear to intend. The issues raised in the submissions might be summarised thus:

a) No franchise holder should be able to hold more than one franchise, instead of two as the White Paper proposes; ownership must also be geographically widespread to prevent the decline of regional culture, production and employment. This point was also raised in relation to the Government's proposals for independent production quotas (see p. 77) and for the Channel 3 arrangements in general (see p. 33);

b) The ITC must have power to prevent takeovers; in any takeover there must be an assessment by the ITC of the buyer's suitability to broadcast, rather than a straight cash sale (arguments here are the same as those relating to the auctioning of franchises – see p. 35).

3. Some submissions offered an assessment of what the White Paper could imply for ownership of television companies in the future:

> Not only does the WP allow a company to have a controlling interest in two C3 licenses (as long as they are in different areas), it also allows that company to be 'domiciled' anywhere in the EC. This makes the C3 licences obvious targets for the media transnationals of Europe.... All these companies have Europe-wide ambitions in TV, and all have the financial muscle to outbid purely domestic rivals in a 'deep pockets' tendering system. Nothing in the WP would prevent all the C3 day-time licences (the ones which will clearly be most lucrative) ending up in the hands of these European media giants. The WP makes a considerable pretence of concern about concentration of ownership, but the controls it offers are either gestural or irrelevant. (Centre for Local Economic Strategies, p. 18)

> 'Real choice could be undermined,' as the Home Secretary has said, 'and opportunities for new broadcasters denied, if British broadcasting were allowed to be dominated by a handful of tycoons or international conglomerates.' (County Natwest Conference, 18 January 1989)

> There can be no discrimination against ownership of television stations passing to other members of the European Community, but ITV does not believe the British people would react positively to the outcome of a highest-bid-wins-all competitive tender that left most of their regional stations in Italian, German, or French hands. British companies are prevented from owning more than 25% of a broadcasting company in France or Spain. Some European countries effectively prevent any shareholding by any company not registered in their own country. The Government's present proposals would permit every regional Channel 3 service to be controlled by non-British interests. ITV submits that it is vital that the cultural and political distinctiveness of Scotland, Wales, Northern Ireland and the regions of England are better protected. The White Paper rightly seeks a widespread ownership in television, and it would be unfortunate if the widespread and regionally-rooted nature of current ITV shareholdings were to be replaced by a number of Channel 3 licensees controlled by single companies not registered in the United Kingdom. (ITV, 9.9–10, p. 65)

a) *Single Franchise Ownership*

4. Most of the submissions were opposed to dual franchise owner-ship, often stressing the effect this could have on the regions:

> ... it is important to ensure that no more than one of the ITV companies is in the same ownership. This is particularly important in the case of the larger companies since, for example, ownership of the two largest companies would give control of 30% of the income and effective control of the network. It would also be an undesirable extension of media power for any national newspaper group to own or control any ITV station. (Television South West, p. 8)

> The White Paper envisages that future legislation will permit Channel 3 franchise holders to have an interest, including a controlling interest, in up to two franchises. We do not seek to comment on this substantive principle; but we wish to see steps taken to ensure that this cannot become a backdoor method of removing a franchise headquarters from our region. Otherwise, the complete merger of two programming services which could potentially result, especially if the primary headquarters were situated outside the region, would effectively leave us with an 'absentee landlord' situation, to the probable detriment of both the region's audience and locally-based independent programme-making interests. (North East Media Development Trust, p. 15)

> Allowing one owner to have two licences could concentrate control of the Channel among seven or eight operators and lead to the closedown of regional stations and loss of local identity.

> The possibility, for example, of a group successfully bidding for Thames and TVS could result in 25% of Channel Three being under one owner. Large operators could 'corner the market' to the detriment of the Channel, the service and particularly, the advertisers....

> In Scotland, this could mean the same group – from anywhere in the EEC – bidding for the two quite different areas of North and Central Scotland. Their intention would be to cut costs by operating from one centre, probably in the Central Belt, and having, at best, minimally staffed satellite studios in the northern area.

> That this could be a publisher contract with no production centres in either area, would have serious implications for both the regional service and for the broadcasting industry in North Scotland....

61

Apart from the loss of direct employment, the symbiotic relationship between the local station and the burgeoning independent sector in the north would go into decline. (Grampian Television, 3.3, p. 13)

5. Advertisers expressed similar concerns:

The IPA wholeheartedly endorses the Government's determination that ownership in the independent television sector should be, and remain, widely spread. The IPA also wishes to emphasise its opposition to any concentration of ownership among the sellers of advertising airtime. In the new broadcasting environment, where the legislative framework will (desirably) be more flexible in allowing access to new companies which may not be themselves licence holders, we are concerned that the control of advertising sales should not be permitted to pass into too few hands. (Institute of Practitioners in Advertising, p. 6)

b) *Takeovers*

There were significant levels of support for the ITC to have powers to block takeovers:

The White Paper while pursuing a diversity of television outlets for Britain also permits takeovers among the regional companies. Over the years a gradual diminution in the number of small companies will take place leaving the more sparsely populated sections of Britain with mere branch plants of larger companies. Even if the ITC prevents regional television falling into the hands of major international organisations, company takeovers will gradually reduce the number of outlets for independent production work within the Channel Three group of companies, as well as the regional benefit derived from local ownership. (British Screen Advisory Council, 6.8, p. 16)

The proposal not to transfer to the ITC the IBA's existing powers to block take-overs must be reconsidered. Without such powers, ITC scrutiny during the allocation of franchises will be rendered meaningless as companies will be able to acquire licences on the Stock Exchange without ITC intervention. (Labour Party, p. 8)

c) *Summary*

7. The general response to this aspect of the Government's proposals may best be summarised by this illustrative example:

The rhetoric of the White Paper is clearly against such concentration of ownership. The specific proposals, unfortunately, lead precisely in that direction (in particular, the possibility of a national newspaper owning two ITV franchises – which could, in the case of Thames and Central, amount to 35% of the ITV network).

We believe that a revised ownership policy should include the following principles:

– No group should control or have undue influence in more than one terrestrial licence of any kind.

– Cross media ownership should be severely restricted and in particular, ownership of national newspapers, satellite services or advertising agencies should be a disqualification for control or undue influence in a terrestrial licence.

– Similarly, terrestrial licence holders should not be able to control or have undue influence in a DBS channel.

– The restrictions on non-EC ownership should be more tightly drawn to prevent attempts to sidestep the regulations (as, for example, in the American intervention in UK cable).

All such regulations need to be precisely drawn and written into the primary legislation. The vague references to the UK of subsequent subordinate legislation are unacceptable – especially, it has to be said, given the deferential attitude so far shown to press mergers. (ACTT, 95–7, p. 27)

8
Programme Standards

The Government's Proposals

1. The Government proposes to put on a statutory footing the recently established Broadcasting Standards Council, the primary function of which is to monitor standards of taste and decency in all television and radio programmes received in the UK, and in video material. The Government also intends to continue its restrictions on television showing statements by Northern Ireland terrorist sympathisers. Here the Government's deregulatory approach is suspended in favour of moral and political regulation. This inconsistency in policy is denied rather than explained: 'Such arrangements are compatible with the proposals to introduce a less regulated framework for broadcasting.' The White Paper argues that the BSC has been established in 'response to the public concern about the portrayal of violence and sex on television'.

The Response

2. Responses were on the whole hostile to the idea of a Broadcasting Standards Council, some citing Professor Peacock's assertion that it 'has no function in a free society'. A range of submissions covered a small number of points:

a) the inconsistency of approach;

b) the lack of evidence of public concern in this matter;

c) the need for the BSC, if it must exist, to concentrate on proper research into broadcasting;

d) the opportunity now provided for a representative consumer body for broadcasting to be established.

a) *The inconsistency of approach*

3. The disparity between a free market approach and the establishment of the BSC was noted by various bodies:

> The Government has chosen to interfere with the free market by appointing the Broadcasting Standards Council, which will reduce the sovereignty of the consumer where matters of taste and decency, and in particular the portrayal of violence and sex, are concerned. As Professor Peacock has commented, 'the new Broadcasting Standards Council amounts to a vote of no confidence in public taste'. (Broadcasting Research Unit, 4.1, p. 9)

> On the one hand, the Government wants to introduce economic deregulation, removing restrictive practices and creating a free marketplace for television. On the other hand, it is profoundly disturbed by the possibility that entrepreneurs may use this freedom to attract audiences through salacious programming of the kind found, for example, in France and the United States.
>
> This is a real problem, but the White Paper gives the impression that yet again the Government has not properly thought through the issues involved. Its apparent solution – to pursue 'light touch' economic deregulation and 'heavy hand' moral re-regulation simultaneously – fails to recognise the practical contradictions which the ITC will face in its work. (Scottish Film Council, 3.8.2–3, p. 8)

> The creation of BSC, with statutory powers, seems unnecessary and wasteful. It seems at odds with the concept of a 'lighter touch' allowed to the new ITC and a system that introduces foreign material to the UK via satellite. (HTV, p. 5)

> ... the Government, having abandoned the regulation which is necessary to preserve high quality programmes and viewers' choice, is introducing a form of regulation which, by all accepted standards, limits the freedom of broadcasting. (Labour Party, p. 15)

b) *The 'public concern' argument*

4. The suggestions that the BSC arose from 'public concern' was questioned by some:

> The White Paper states 'recently there has been much public concern about the portrayal of violence and sex in broadcast

65

programmes, especially on television' (7.3), and it argues that special safeguards are needed to meet public concern. Having reviewed all the relevant research into public attitudes in this area, the BRU can state with confidence that there is no evidence of public concern being very substantial or rising in a significant manner. (Broadcasting Research Unit, 4.2, p. 9)

Sex and violence are clearly issues of great concern to some viewers; but there are many other issues not within the current remit which research has shown to be of far greater concern to more people – particularly the entertainment value of programmes, and the extent of viewer satisfaction with the range of and choices of programmes on offer. One concern is that, if the BSC is to stay as it is, it will be increasingly marginal to the continuing debate about the future shape of television. (Consumers' Association, 10.2, p. 20)

... the IBA's latest (October 1988) annual survey on attitudes to broadcasting included the following results:

– 60% of respondents had not seen anything at all offensive on television
– offensive material reported declined by 5% and viewers were offended less frequently
– as sources of offence, violence decreased by 5% and sex by 3%
– more significant criticisms were about the number of repeats and about 'bad language'
– 70% reported that programmes had improved or stayed the same
– only 1 in 20 or less respondents cited sex or violence as a source of complaint. (ACTT, 108, p. 29–30)

c) *The role of the BSC*

5. Commentators scrutinised the likely functions of the BSC, with some concluding that it should be wound up immediately; others suggesting that it should draw up a code and then disappear; others again wishing to limit its remit; and still others advocating that it should be reformed into a consultative consumer body:

There is a danger, given the narrow interpretation of its remit to oversee 'standards', that the Council may seek for itself a wider remit and hence wider powers. It has already been suggested that

66

the Council might monitor programme diversity and the continued provision of minority programmes. Such positive programming obligations are a very necessary regulatory function which should be in the hands of the sovereign regulatory body, the Independent Television Commission. The body which has the power to issue and rescind franchises must have responsibility for monitoring the performance of contractors to ensure they are fulfilling their franchise commitments. To separate these functions would be organisational nonsense. (Broadcasting Research Unit, 4.5, p. 10)

The British Film Institute strongly believes that there is no need to introduce a statutory code for broadcasting. What is required is a system of broadcasting so regulated as to create a context for the maintenance of the high standards of responsibility currently operative, and which have made British TV so widely admired throughout the world.

It is important that the end product after the introduction of the new regulatory framework should represent the public's best interest as well as commercial concerns. Much will be lost if the proposals in this area are reactive and negative. It ought to be possible to sustain the diversity and richness of present day television and to ensure that standards are not undercut by programming that offers the lowest levels of entertainment and information. . . .

If the Broadcasting Standards Council is established by statute, it should have a remit restricted to retrospective comment. It should have no powers to preview material. Any code it produces should be advisory and not mandatory. (BFI, 5.1–5.5, pp. 17–18)

VoL has repeatedly called for the establishment of a representative, Consultative Consumer Body, and for a National Commission on Broadcasting charged with the duty of monitoring and reviewing every aspect and development of relevance to the industry and of presenting an annual 'state of the nation' report to Government and Parliament.

VoL sees the BSC fulfilling neither of these roles in its present form. VoL believes however that the BSC might well be the embryo of such a national commission provided its terms of reference and its status are changed once it has discharged its current duty of drawing up a code of practice.

It would be most important for the new commission to be seen in a positive, not negative, role and the BSC could not be charged with the duties of such a commission so long as it was required to lay down codes of conduct. (Voice of the Listener, 11.3–5, p. 16)

In relation to its size and importance, no other area of public life is so obviously lacking a proper representation of the public interest. Both the BBC and ITV have a host of advisory committees, but they are 'grace and favour' groupings, whose organisation, agenda and perspectives are largely set by the broadcasters. They should be replaced with a BCC funded from general taxation, and operating at arms length from both the government and the broadcasters. (Centre for Local Economic Strategies, p. 46)

d) *The need for research*

6. A large body of evidence stressed that, if the BSC were to continue, its role should be to conduct proper research, particularly as the IBA's current research function might be lost under the Government's proposals for Channel 3:

Looking forward, we are concerned that there should be, within the system, a continued facility for high-quality consumer research in the broadcasting field. For example, when the criteria for awarding Channel 3 franchises are set up, these need to be based on the best possible evidence of how well individual companies, and the system as a whole, is performing. It is in the public interest that this kind of work should be done – especially given the proposal not to replace the IBA's research function – but it is clear that the market system alone will not support it.

We do not have any strong views about where this research capacity should be located, though it must be completely independent from both the Government and the industry – and (we would submit) the proposed Independent Television Corporation, whose role we would see confined mainly to licensing and regulation. One possibility would be to place this responsibility with the Broadcasting Standards Council; another to establish a separate Broadcasting Foundation, financed by a levy on the companies. (Consumers' Association, 14.3–4, p. 10)

We suggest that the BSC should use the mechanism of an annual report to Parliament to publish a researched and considered analysis of the content of the previous year's British Television programming using a set of objective performance criteria which will enable a year-on-year comparison of the range, scope and tenor of programmes, and how standards of taste and decency are both shifting and being interpreted. (BFI, 5.6, p. 18)

7. The BSC itself shared this view:

The Council believes that, as an extension of its existing role in the Government's provision of consumer protection, it could play a part in the wider field of research into the attitudes of the public towards broadcasting and the effects of broadcasting within different sections of the population. The IBA has hitherto maintained a significant proportion of the existing research effort of the broadcasters, but if no similar obligations lie on the ITC and the Radio Authority, then public understanding of the broadcasting services would be diminished proportionately. (Broadcasting Standards Council, 13, p. 6)

e) *Government censorship*

8. Finally, some submissions also criticised the Government's censorship of issues relating to Northern Ireland:

We opposed at the time, and we continue to oppose, the government's decision in October 1988 on broadcasts by representatives of or groups sympathetic with terrorist organisations connected with Northern Ireland. We believe that this was a gross abuse in peacetime of the reserve powers of direction that the government has always had. We do not accept the bald statement that appearances by representatives of terrorist organisations had caused offence to many viewers and listeners and had provided a public platform to propagate terrorism. The government's decision has dangerous political and legal implications, has caused severe practical difficulties for the broadcasters, has contributed significantly to the increase of censorship by, or fostered by, government and has damaged, and will continue to damage, the reputation of British broadcasters at home and abroad for fair and impartial news reporting. (BETA, 49, p. 17)

We have never been convinced of the need for such Government interference and we are alarmed that 'such powers' should be continued by Government. (Writers' Guild, 7.15)

9
Radio

The Government's Proposals

1. The Government's plans for radio are set out only in outline in the White Paper, as a Green Paper was issued in 1987. Broadly, it is proposed to establish a 'slim' Radio Authority to license and monitor new local independent commercial stations; in addition, three new national commercial stations are to be established. The BBC will continue to provide public service broadcasting, although the arrangements for its funding after the licence fee has been phased out are left unstated in the White Paper. The White Paper also says that public authority funding will not generally be available to stations.

The Response

2. Many responses did not concern themselves with, or only touched upon, the radio proposals. Those that addressed the issues focused on two main points:

a) the White Paper's ambiguity about the future security of BBC radio funding;

b) the need to permit local authority support for community radio.

3. The Voice of the Listener, in its submission, added that the BBC should retain a strong presence on all frequencies and that national commercial radio should follow a public service pattern of broadcasting. Other submissions stressed that the new stations should be required to broadcast drama, news and other quality programmes.

a) *The future of BBC Radio*

4. The uncertain future of BBC Radio in a post-licence fee environment concerned a few of the bodies whose evidence we reviewed:

BBC Radio makes an incalculable contribution to the cultural and community life of the nation at national and local level. It must be assured of adequate funding and frequencies to do its job properly. BBC Radio currently gets 27% of the BBC's licence fee income. The White Paper, in setting the BBC the objective of moving to subscription television, merely states that 'account will need to be taken in due course of the implications for financing BBC radio services'. This is simply not good enough. (Voice of the Listener, summary p. 3)

But once the television licence fee, out of which BBC Radio services are funded, is replaced by television subscription there is no provision for funding BBC radio at all. 'Taking account of this in due course' is simply not good enough in these days of rapid technological change and development when any broadcasting organisation must be able to plan at least ten years ahead in formulating policy. (Writers' Guild, annex)

It is not at all clear what will happen to BBC Radio in the long term in the context of the Government's wish to phase out the licence fee. A change to subscription services will presumably provide revenue only for BBC Television. As they stand the Government's proposals seem to make the future of BBC Radio very precarious. (Society of Authors)

b) *Community Radio and Public Funding*

5. The proscription of local authority support for community radio was opposed by some:

... the financial requirements of bidding for and successfully establishing a community radio will effectively disenfranchise those communities which these services are ostensibly there to serve. The Forum would therefore welcome a revision of Government's restrictions on local authority assistance towards the establishment of community radio stations, which seems to run counter to Government's policy of promoting the development of community enterprises within the Inner City. (Birmingham Media Training Forum, 6, p. 6)

There is concern, however, at suggestions in the White Paper that organisations bidding for community radio franchises will not be able to utilise public sector finance. GLA made a strong case in its response to the 1987 Green Paper that the arts in particular would benefit from support to community radio licensees from Regional Arts Associations, local authorities and other development agencies, and we had understood that such a role had been accepted by the Government.

We hope that legislation will be framed to ensure that public authority finance of this sort can be utilised where there is a clear benefit to the community. (Greater London Arts, 6, p. 6)

c) *The advertisers' views*

6. Advertisers sounded a note of caution about any proliferation of new commercial stations:

> ... but we must point out that the opportunity of raising advertising revenue in a more competitive field may not be as great as optimistic applicants for these services may assume. We believe, therefore, that the Radio Authority should be set up as early as possible, with the ability to guide applicants about the commercial skills which they will need. (Incorporated Society of British Advertisers, 13, p. 6)

7. These views were shared, perhaps not surprisingly, by at least one local radio station, which feared that there would be insufficient advertising revenue to sustain the full range of proposed services, including independent local radio:

> The sharp drop in radio's national advertising revenue only a few years ago, from £39 million to £33 million, is attributed by many to increased advertising on Channel 4. There is no evidence to indicate that advertising revenue will grow in proportion to the number of new services introduced. Some of these may attract not enough revenue to survive but just enough to damage the viability of some existing services. It is vital, therefore, that the pace at which new services are introduced is carefully geared to the likely availability of finance. (Radio Clyde, p. 1)

10
Transmission

The Government's Proposals

1. The Government intend to privatise the transmission services for broadcasting, moving to a series of regionally based, private transmission operators. The purpose is to introduce competition into this part of the broadcasting environment. The White Paper acknowledges the very high standards achieved under existing arrangements and hopes that these can be maintained after the changes. This then is not a reform aimed at improving current performance but simply a desire to open the market for private operators, reflecting political preferences.

As is reported earlier, on 4 July 1989, the Home Secretary announced the Government's proposals in this area. The transmission networks are to be privatised, but not on the lines suggested in the White Paper of a series of local operators. Instead, the existing BBC and IBA networks were to be retained and sold to two private operators working on a national basis. The BBC would sell its network after 1996; the IBA would sell its network once the Bill was in force. Tariffs would be set at levels reflecting the percentage of total Channel 3 income received by each individual franchise holder. The Director General of Telecommunications would be empowered to regulate the new system to ensure fairness and maintenance of standards.

The Response

2. There was widespread opposition to the original proposals, which can be broken down into the following main strands:

  – there is no justification for changing the existing arrangements, which are working well;

– a market approach to transmission would endanger present arrangements, whereby the cost of transmitting to the more remote areas is subsidised by the more populated regions, and thus universality would be jeopardised;

– any regional supplier would hold a monopoly of delivery in that area and could thus dictate to the programme suppliers – competition is neither possible nor desirable.

a) *The need for change?*

3. A number of submissions questioned the need for change here at all:

> Consumers' Association does not normally take a view on the principles of privatisation....
>
> But we confess to being baffled by the Government's proposals on privatising the transmission system. It is a natural monopoly delivering services to very nearly the entire population, at very low cost and with a high standard of service. It is hard to see how any meaningful element of competition could be introduced, but equally it is hard to see that the returns from privatisation would justify the establishment of a new regulatory mechanism with (presumably) its own staff and resources to oversee, for example, the maintenance of technical standards. (Consumers' Association, 11.2–3, p. 21)

b) *Transmission to the remoter regions*

4. A large number of submissions drew attention to the need for cross-subsidies within the transmission system if remoter regions were to continue to receive an adequate service:

> The proposal for the privatisation of transmitters contained in paras. 9.1–9.2 of the White Paper is potentially devastating for a terrestrial television service in Wales. Because of the topography of Wales, it is impossible to provide adequate terrestrial coverage without a disproportionately large number of transmitters. Under the present system of cross subsidy it is possible to maintain almost complete coverage. S4C, like Channel 4, makes no payment for the use of the transmitters at present, but if these were privatised, presumably payment would or could be demanded and the cost could well be high. This would increase further the amount of

subsidy needed to fund S4C and would render an 'S4C Subscription' even more vulnerable. (S4C, 6.29, p. 19)

Given that the present arrangements allow ITV to reach all parts of the country, with the largest and richest regions subsidising the more sparsely-populated and more difficult terrains, it is difficult to see what benefits will flow from this proposal.

While there may be scope for reducing costs and improving service through competition, it is not easy to see how a private enterprise scheme could operate a necessarily sensitive arrangement which could accommodate both the 'cross-subsidy' and the 'ability to pay' features which are part of the present system. (BFI, 12.1–2, p. 25)

South West Arts is concerned that proposals to privatise the transmission system currently maintained by the IBA (9.2, 9.4) could have adverse effects on a largely rural region with a scattered population such as our own. The areas currently serviced by HTV West and TSW require a total of 120 transmitters to reach the region's population, and the region therefore currently benefits from the 'cross-subsidy' system operated by the IBA. We are concerned that private operators would view this system as uneconomic and that the quality of service in the rural parts of the region might therefore be threatened. (South West Arts, 8)

c) *The IBA view*

5. One submission supported the principle of privatisation, but stressed the need to maintain national, integrated systems which allowed for cross-subsidisation where necessary:

The commitment in the White Paper to universality for Channels 3 and 4, and to the national character of the fifth channel, makes a fragmented transmission system more complex and less efficient to operate than the present integrated system. Moreover, because of the diversity of skills and resources required in transmission operations, fragmentation would provide lower economies of scale in staff utilisation, spares holdings and purchase of plant, besides requiring extra coordination in communications and transmission monitoring. Relationships and tariff negotiations with other major service providers (e.g. electricity and telecommunications) are more efficient in an integrated system, as are the major project works associated with engineering improvements, such as the conversion of television transmitters to carry stereo sound channels.

The Government's objectives would be more effectively and speedily achieved, with less risk of deterioration in reliability, technical quality or increase in costs, by privatising the IBA and BBC transmission operations separately, without fragmenting them. (IBA, 9.5–6, p. 57)

d) *The absence of competition*

6. A smaller range of submissions questioned the scope for real competition in the supply of transmission services:

We assume that there will not be two or more transmitters on offer to the broadcaster at every site, so in effect for any one transmitter reception area, the broadcaster will be in the hands of a monopoly supplier. How then can competition be promoted, as proposed in the White Paper? Safeguards will be required through the medium of the contract between broadcaster and transmitter contractor to ensure acceptable technical performance, including speed of repair and maintenance. This is an area where time truly is money. But will not the monopoly supplier be in an unacceptably strong position? Will that not be a worse situation than to be in the hands of a public authority (the IBA/ITC) which has the reputation and the skills acquired over many years? (Scottish Television, p. 6)

We do not understand in what sense a 'competitive transmission industry' is possible. The extent of economies of scale in relation to demand suggests that the present system has the characteristics of a natural monopoly. One could not envisage alternative transmission systems operating at any given time which would offer a choice to each Channel Three licensee, given the nature of the transmitter system. . . .

The proposal to privatise the transmission system also raises considerable problems. Given its natural monopoly position it would be able to extract monopoly profits from the Channel Three licensees (which would in turn reduce the auction proceeds for the Government), and provisionally from the BBC also. An elaborate framework of price regulation would be required to avoid this occurring, and the advantages of vertical integration would be lost. (TVS, 4.1, pp. 21–2)

11
Programme Production

The Government's Proposals

1. The Government have already imposed quotas on the BBC and IBA to secure 25 per cent of programme production from independent producers, rather than in-house, by 1993. The Government envisage further opportunities for the independent sector following the deregulation of broadcasting after 1992. No ITC franchise holder will be required to produce programmes, and so may commission work from independents on a larger scale than at present. The intention here is to promote the growth of independent producers and to counter the 'excessive degree of vertical integration' in the broadcasting industry, which the Government believe has created inefficiency.

The Response

2. Although there was general support for this encouragement of independent production, some concerns were voiced. A general concern, discussed earlier (see pp. 35–6), was that the intense financial pressures on all terrestrial broadcasters after 1992 would force them to import programmes rather than produce any indigenous material. More specific points raised were:

a) organisations representing independent producers wished to see tighter enforcement of the 25 per cent quotas;

b) various bodies stressed the need to secure a wide range of independent producers, rather than a small number of larger companies taking the lion's share of commissions;

c) a number of submissions emphasised the need to preserve regional independent production.

a) *The Producers' Views*

3. Independent production companies were concerned to see the 25 per cent quotas enforced:

> It will be amongst the duties of the ITC to ensure that Channel 3 franchisees meet the 25% target for independent access set by the Government. It is clear that some franchisees will achieve and surpass the target more easily and willingly than others. IPPA has not been impressed by the IBA's record of implementing the Government's independent access objective. We do not believe that the IBA has acted effectively in this regard. We assume that, in contrast to the IBA, the ITC will regulate in favour of competition and fair trading practices. We are convinced that effective, independent monitoring is essential if the 25% target is to be achieved. We also believe this supervision should extend beyond counting hours and adding up programme expenditure, to encompass ownership questions and competition issues. We would suggest that the ability of the ITC to implement the Government's 25% policy might be enhanced by the appointment of an independent evaluator with responsibility to oversee all issues relating to independent access to all UK television channels. (Independent Programme Producers, 3.4, p. 6)

b) *Securing a wide production base*

4. The need to spread commissions across a wide production base was stressed in various submissions:

> Since a monopolistic situation may arise ... in the supply of material for transmission ... no ITC licence holder should be able to acquire more than 20% of its programme material from a single company. ... Similarly, of the 25% of its programmes which each ITC company will be required to obtain from independent producers, no more than 20% should be derived from a single company. (Sussex University Broadcasting Group, 5.5, pp. 6–7)

c) *Preserving regional production*

5. The regional aspect of independent production featured in a number of submissions, often allied with the widely perceived threat to regional programmes presented by the White Paper's proposals for Channel 3 in general:

... a commitment to locally-based independent production should be an obligation laid on licensees. If this condition is not laid down, the 25% from independent producers could eventually consist entirely of international co-productions: the 1990s versions of *Dallas* and *Dynasty*. We believe that this is not what the Government intends, but unless action is taken in advance it may be what the Government allows by default. (Scottish Film Council, 3.6.2, p. 7)

Recognising the Government's desire to foster greater competition, the Forum would like to see support for a clearly defined regional 'independent' production sector in order to ensure that programme-making does not become monophonistic in character. The White Paper gives more attention to competition in relation to programme delivery; however a genuine increase in customer choice and programme variety can only be sustained by a diverse production base. The encouragement of a strong regionally-based production sector is an effective means of avoiding excessive concentration of ownership, and extending programme diversity. (Birmingham Media Training Forum, 4.2, p. 5)

[The White Paper] clears the way for the ITC to reduce the number and increase the size of transmission areas, whilst making entirely rhetorical noises about 'regionalism'.... The other critical factor will be the WP's all-clear for C3 licensees to contract out all their programme supply ... this could literally decimate the 25 year old production system of ITV. In a weakly regulated 'free market' model of the sort the WP envisages, the benefits of an expansion of independent production will be heavily concentrated in London. Nothing in the WP suggests that the C3 model will require more than a token amount of genuinely regional output. (Centre for Local Economic Strategies, p. 28)

12
Omissions

A number of additional points arose in the evidence surveyed. These issues do not fall into any one of the categories suggested by the White Paper's chapter headings. Accordingly, we have presented them here in a separate section.

Training

The most frequently mentioned omission from the White Paper was the provision of training under the new dispensation. Many submissions argued that the increased use of independent commissions in the future will lead to a fragmented and casualised production base, with little incentive for the ITV companies to invest in training. Further, the new financial pressures on the commercial companies and on the BBC will reduce the resources available for training in any event. Thus, submissions argued, proper provision for training should be established:

> Broadcasting depends on the availability of a skilled workforce. But the White Paper makes no mention of training. The broadcasting authorities have always recognised their responsibility for training their staff and the BBC has a particularly good record in this field. The financial pressures on the BBC, however, are bound to affect its ability to sustain its training programme. It seems unlikely that the ITC will take training seriously. There is no reason at all to believe that, in the absence of a powerful regulatory body and in the market conditions in which they will be expected to operate, channels 3, 4 and 5 or DBS voluntarily will undertake serious training commitments. A positive requirement, therefore, to establish effective training arrangements in co-operation with the relevant trades unions must be imposed on the broadcasting authorities and the programme companies. (BETA, 52, p. 18)

The White Paper does not address the question of training in the television industry. The new environment will increase the amount of freelance and independent activity, whilst at the same time putting financial pressure on established broadcasters to reduce the amount of training they undertake. There is a real danger of an upsurge in demand for skilled labour which cannot be met, leading to inflationary pressures, restrictions on the growth of independent production, and the transfer of production overseas. We suggest that it would be beneficial, to the industry as a whole, if all channels whose services originate within the United Kingdom were obliged to contribute a specified percentage of revenue to a central training fund, administered by the industry's employers. (Channel 4, 6.8, p. 26)

... the advanced technology used in the television industry makes training particularly expensive: it has been said that the cost is second only to that of training aeroplane pilots. It seems likely that some support from the public purse will continue to be required ... If the industry is to continue making a financial contribution to the cost of training along with the public purse, then one possible source is a proportion of the advertising levy on broadcasters. ... Overall the period of the changes in broadcasting heralded by the White Paper is the appropriate moment for the Government to satisfy itself that one of the crucial ingredients of the new mixture – training for independent programme production, and the financial underpinning of that training – is securely in place to meet future needs. (North East Media Development Trust, 23)

We are disappointed that the proposals make no mention of the need for a continued commitment to training by broadcasters and suggest that a requirement to provide finance for training should be included for all contract applicants. Anglia Television regards such a commitment, which could be monitored by the ITC, as an essential element in the safeguarding of quality. (Anglia Television, 6.1)

Feature film production

The BFI drew attention to the relationship between television and feature film production:

An important development in the last few years has been the growth of subsidiary companies of the ITV system involved in

81

making Feature Films. These films have often had a successful theatrical life, and have gained prizes at festivals and a world-wide reputation for the UK.

The BBC has recently become involved in a similar enterprise, and has started to invest in feature-length productions.

This activity has increasingly provided the only chance for British personnel to be involved in feature film production.

Any reduction in funds for production in the television sector would have an adverse effect on this development. We believe it to be vital to the continuation of Feature Film-making in this country that this activity should be protected.

We recommend that consideration is given to the possibility of providing fiscal advantages within the levy calculations for Companies who decide to set up film-making companies of this type, or who choose to make a contribution to the public bodies supporting film production, such as the BFI and the Scottish Film Production Fund. We also recommend that potential franchise holders who have plans for development in this area should be given priority. (BFI, 13.1–5, p. 26)

Archiving

The question of preserving the heritage of television was not referred to in the White Paper but was dealt with in two submissions:

The proliferation of channels and the likely increase in the number of production companies, together with a more complex copyright environment, has turned the need for a National TV Archive from a desirable objective into an urgent necessity. At the same time, the recent Copyright Designs and Patents legislation has opened up the opportunity for the BFI to undertake this role. . . .

The IBA currently requires franchise holders, including BSB, to make appropriate archival provision for their broadcast material. . . . We would recommend that a similar provision be imposed statutorily on all companies wishing to bid for franchises in the new system.

The current arrangements negotiated through the ITVA and Channel 4 include payment of the direct costs of making the present level of recording. The ITVA annual grant to the BFI also covers the collection of appropriate documentation, and of stills. Some system to provide this funding over all channels will need to be devised in future if this work is to continue. Indeed it could be argued that in a highly competitive deregulated system the broadcasters may have neither the resources nor the inclination to make even the current level of provision. It may be necessary therefore for the Government to require the ITC to include such a condition within the positive programming obligations, and to require the BBC to guarantee its contribution. (BFI, 6.2, 6.6–7, pp. 19–20)

... the scale of present and future output means that no constant monitoring can be undertaken at an economic cost. The Council believes, therefore, that it requires powers to ensure that, within a reasonable period after transmission, it can have access to a programme which may be the subject of its enquiries. It proposes therefore that the BBC and the companies licensed by the IBA/ITC/ Radio Authority should be required to retain copies of all broadcast material for a minimum period, whether originated live or as recordings in some form. The requirement on the television organisations could in part be met, as things stand at present, by means of the British Film Institute Archive. With the exception of the Scottish Film Council, the Institute is the only body currently designated by the DTI, under the Copyright Act, 1988, to retain recordings without copyright charges. (Broadcasting Standards Council, p. 5)

Appendix

The following is a list of organisations whose submissions in response to the Government's White Paper were consulted in the preparation of this monograph.

Anglia Television
Association of Cinematograph, Television and Allied Technicians
BACTV (British Action for Children's Television)
BBC
Birmingham Media Training Forum
British Film and Television Producers' Association
British Film Institute
British Satellite Broadcasting
British Screen Advisory Council
Broadcasting and Entertainment Trades Alliance
Broadcasting Research Unit
Broadcasting Standards Council
Campaign for Press and Broadcasting Freedom
Campaign for Quality Television
Central Independent Television
Centre for Local Economic Strategies
Channel 4
Church of England General Synod
Consumers' Association
Grampian Television
Greater London Arts Association
HTV
Independent Broadcasting Authority
Independent Television Association
Incorporated Society of British Advertisers
Institute of Practitioners in Advertising

IPPA
Labour Party
Mersey Television
National Association of Head Teachers
National Campaign for the Arts
National Union of Journalists
North East Media Development Trust
Scottish Film Council
Scottish Television
S4C
Society of Authors
South West Arts Association
Sussex University Broadcasting Group
Television South
Television South West
Thames Television
Voice of the Listener
Writers' Guild of Great Britain
Yorkshire Arts
Yorkshire Television